Handy Reference

Office as a whole		Word	[illegible]	[illegible]	[illegible]	[illegible]
Create new document	Ctrl+N	✔	[illegible]	[illegible]	[illegible]	[illegible]
Open existing document	Ctrl+O	✔	[illegible]	[illegible]	[illegible]	[illegible]
Save active document	Ctrl+S	✔	[illegible]	[illegible]	[illegible]	[illegible]
Print active document	Ctrl+P	✔	✔	[illegible]	[illegible]	[illegible]
Embolden text	Ctrl+B	✔	✔	✔		
Italicises text	Ctrl+I	✔	✔	✔		
Underline text	Ctrl+U	✔	✔	✔		
Left-align text	Ctrl+L	✔		✔		
Right-align text	Ctrl+R	✔		✔		
Justify text	Ctrl+J	✔		✔		
Centre text	Ctrl+E	✔		✔		
Find	Ctrl+F	✔	✔	✔		
Find-and-replace	Ctrl+H	✔	✔	✔		
Select All	Ctrl+A	✔	✔			
Undo action	Ctrl+Z	✔	✔	✔		✔
Redo action	Ctrl+Y	✔	✔			

Word	
Activate Font button	Ctrl+Shift+F
Activate Font Size button	Ctrl+Shift+P
Indent text	Ctrl+M
Print Preview	Ctrl+F2
Spelling & grammar check	F7
Thesaurus	Shift+F7
Excel	
Select row	Shift+Space
Select column	Ctrl+Space
Toggle Selection mode	F8
Launch Edit mode	F2
Launch Paste Function dialog	Shift+F3
Launch Format Cells dialog	Ctrl+1
Insert current date	Ctrl+;
Insert current time	Ctrl+Shift+;
Spelling check	F7
AutoRoute Express	
Launch Find dialog	Ctrl+G
Zoom out/in	F5/F6
Launch Route Wizard	Ctrl+R
Close route	Ctrl+L

Publisher	
Move to start of text frame	Ctrl+Home
Move to end of text frame	Ctrl+End
Move to next linked frame	Ctrl+Shift+Enter
Highlight active text frame	Ctrl+A
Copy text formatting	Ctrl+Shift+C
Paste text formatting	Ctrl+Shift+V
Increase font size by 1 point	Ctrl+]
Decrease font size by 1 point	Ctrl+[
Spelling check	F7
Add shadow to object	Ctrl+D
Group/ungroup objects	Ctrl+Shift+G
Add new page	Ctrl+Shift+N
Reverse Undo	Ctrl+Z
Outlook	
Launch new item (in folder)	Ctrl+N
Launch Inbox	Ctrl+Shift+I
Launch Outbox	Ctrl+Shift+O
Check for new mail	F5
Launch Find dialog	Ctrl+Shift+F
Create new document	Ctrl+Shift+H
Reverse Undo	Ctrl+Z

About the Series

In easy steps series is developed for time-sensitive people who want results fast. It is designed for quick, easy and effortless learning.

By using the best authors in the field, combined with our in-house expertise in computing, this series is ideal for all computer users. It explains the essentials simply, concisely and clearly - without the unnecessary verbal blurb. We strive to ensure that each book is technically superior, effective for easy learning and offers the best value.

Learn the essentials **in easy steps** - accept no substitutes!

Titles in the series include:

Operating Systems	
Windows 95	1- 874029-28-8
Windows CE	1-874029-80-6
Applications – Integrated	
Microsoft Office 97	1-874029-66-0
Microsoft Office	1-874029-37-7
Microsoft Office SBE	1-874029-81-4
Microsoft Works	1-874029-41-5
SmartSuite (97)	1-874029-67-9
Graphics and Desktop Publishing	
CorelDRAW	1-874029-72-5
PageMaker	1-874029-35-0
PagePlus	1-874029-49-0
Photoshop	1-874029-82-2
Publisher	1-874029-77-6
Development Tools	
Visual Basic	1-874029-74-1
Visual J++	1-874029-75-X
Hardware	
Upgrading Your PC	1-874029-76-8

Applications – General	
Access	1-874029-78-4
Excel	1-874029-69-5
PowerPoint	1-874029-63-6
Word 97	1-874029-68-7
Word	1-874029-39-3
WordPerfect	1-874029-59-8
Internet	
CompuServe UK	1-874029-33-4
FrontPage	1-874029-60-1
HTML	1-874029-46-6
Internet Explorer 4	1-874029-84-9
Internet UK	1-874029-73-3
Netscape Navigator	1-874029-47-4
Accounting and Finance	
Microsoft Money UK	1-874029-61-X
QuickBooks UK	1-874029-83-0
Quicken UK	1-874029-71-7
Sage Instant Accounting	1-874029-44-X
Sage Sterling for Windows	1-874029-79-2

For credit card sales and volume discounts Tel: 01926 817999 or EMail: sales@computerstep.com

For international orders and rights Fax: +44 1926 817005 or EMail: sevanti@computerstep.com

EMail your reader comments to: harshad@computerstep.com

Visit our web site at http://www.computerstep.com

MICROSOFT OFFICE SMALL BUSINESS EDITION in easy steps

Stephen Copestake

COMPUTER STEP

In easy steps is an imprint of Computer Step
Southfield Road . Southam
Warwickshire CV33 OFB . England

Tel: 01926 817999 Fax: 01926 817005
http://www.computerstep.com

First published 1997

Printed and bound in the United Kingdom

ISBN 1-874029-81-4

Contents

3 Excel 79

Chapter One

First Steps

This chapter shows you how to get started quickly in Office – Small Business Edition. You'll learn to work with toolbars; create new documents with templates and wizards; and open/save existing documents (on your hard disk and on the Internet). Finally, you'll learn how to get information you need from Office's on-line HELP system (including Office Assistant).

Covers

Introduction

The Small Business Edition of Microsoft Office contains these modules:

- Word — word-processor
- Excel — spreadsheet
- Publisher — desktop publishing module
- AutoRoute Express — route planner
- Outlook — personal/business information manager

Word and Excel share a common look and feel, while Outlook, Publisher and AutoRoute Express – although they necessarily adopt a more or less individualistic approach – integrate well with themselves and the other modules. (For example, you can easily copy map sections from AutoRoute Express to Publisher, and Word can act as Outlook's e-mail editor).

The illustration below shows the Word opening screen. Flagged are components which are common to Publisher, Outlook and Excel, too.

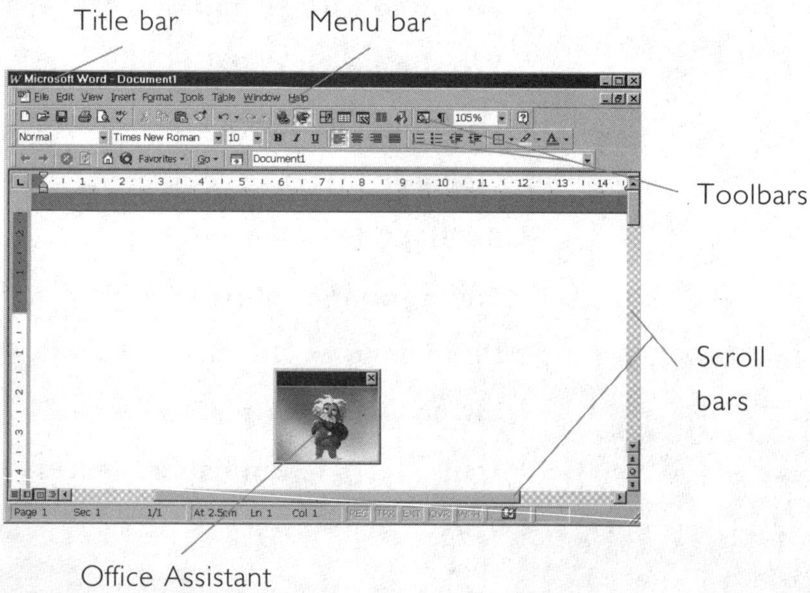

REMEMBER

There are, of course, differences between the module screens; we'll explore these in later chapters.

REMEMBER

The AutoRoute Express screen is quite distinct – for more information, see Chapter Five.

REMEMBER

You can't use the Office Assistant in Publisher and AutoRoute Express.

REMEMBER

For more information on the use of the Office Assistant, see pages 23-26.

Toolbars

HANDY TIP

To add a new button to a toolbar in Word or Excel, right-click over the toolbar. Click Customize. In the dialog which launches, click the Commands tab. In the Categories field, click a category (a group of associated icons). In the Commands box, drag a button onto the toolbar *in the open document*. Finally, click Close.

Toolbars are important components in all Office modules apart from AutoRoute Express. A toolbar is an on-screen bar which contains shortcut buttons. These symbolise and allow easy access to often-used commands which would normally have to be invoked via one or more menus.

For example, Word's Standard toolbar lets you:

- create, open, save and print documents
- perform copy & paste and cut & paste operations
- undo editing actions
- access Word's Help system

by simply clicking on the relevant button.

Toolbars vary to some extent from module to module. We'll be looking at these in more detail as we encounter them. For the moment, some general advice.

Specifying which toolbars are displayed

In any Office module, pull down the View menu and click Toolbars. Now do the following:

HANDY TIP

Outlook and Publisher only have two toolbars. AutoRoute Express has none.

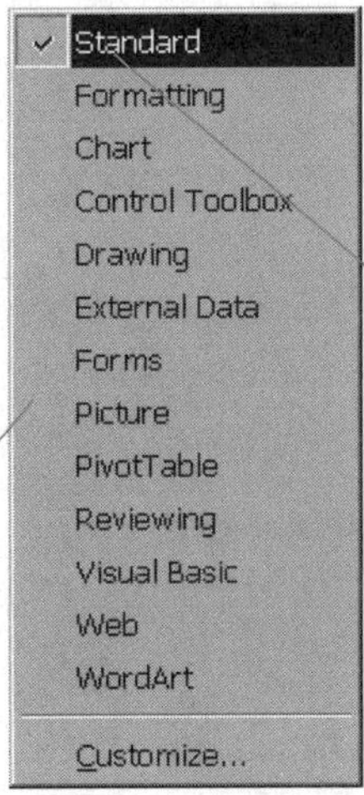

Click the toolbar you want to be visible – a ✔ appears against it

REMEMBER

This is Excel's toolbar list. Available toolbars in Word, Publisher, Excel and Outlook vary.

Repeat this procedure for as many toolbars as necessary.

Creating new documents

REMEMBER **Because Word, Publisher and Excel are reasonably uniform in the way they create new documents, we'll look at this topic here rather than in later, module-specific chapters.**

With the exception of Outlook and AutoRoute Express, all Office modules let you:

- create new blank documents
- create new documents based on a 'template'
- create new documents with the help of a 'Wizard'

Creating blank documents is the simplest route to new document creation; use this if you want to define the document components yourself from scratch. This is often not the most efficient or effective way to create new documents.

Templates – also known as boilerplates – are sample documents complete with the relevant formatting and/or text. By basing a new document on a template, you automatically have access to these.

Wizards are advanced templates which incorporate a question-and-answer system. You work through a series of dialogs, answering the appropriate questions and making the relevant choices.

Documents created with the use of templates or Wizards can easily be amended subsequently.

Both templates and Wizards are high-powered yet easy-to-use shortcuts to document creation. Office provides a large number of templates and Wizards. For example, Word offers Wizards which automate the production of newsletters, faxes, letters and memos, as well as numerous templates.

REMEMBER **Topics which relate to the New dialog, templates and Wizards do not apply to Outlook and AutoRoute Express.**

All three document creation methods involve launching the New dialog (although Publisher has its own version). This can be accessed:

- from within the modified Windows Start menu
- from within the relevant Office program

Launching the New dialog

Utilise either of the following methods:

Using the Start menu

When Office is installed, it amends the Windows Start menu. Carry out the following procedure:

You can't use the Start menu route to create a new Publisher document.

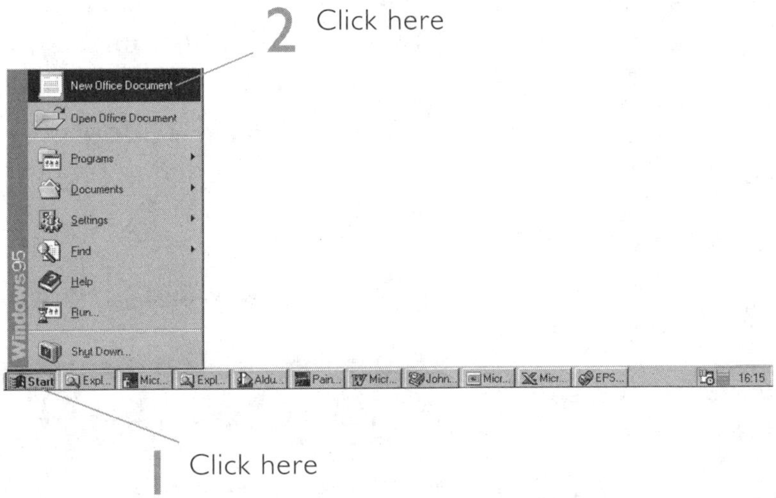

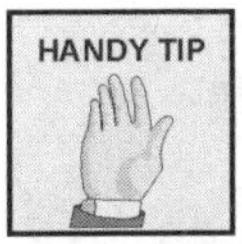

In Publisher, click Create New Publication in the File menu.

From within the program

In Word or Excel, pull down the File menu and do the following:

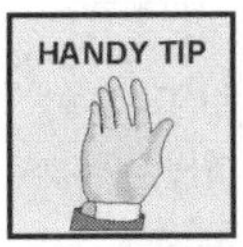

The following keyboard shortcut is available in Word and Excel. Simply press Ctrl+N.

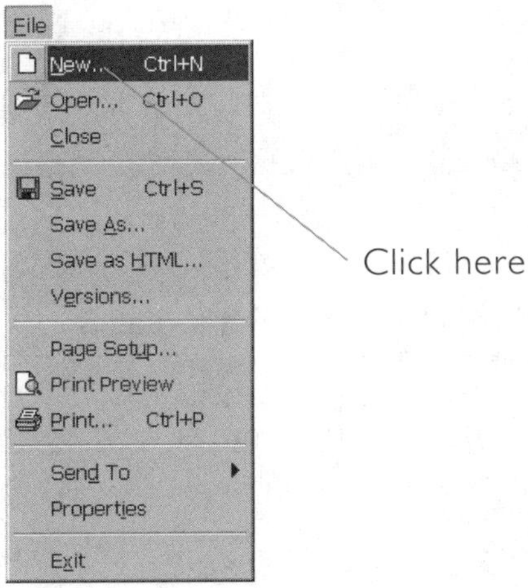

Using the New dialog (1)

HANDY TIP

In Publisher, the New dialog looks different. Do the following:

A Click here

B Double-click any wizard

Alternatively, to create a *blank* Publisher document, click the Blank Page tab, then double-click any blank page icon.

REMEMBER

To create a blank document in Word or Excel, activate the General tab and click the Blank Document (Word) or Blank Workbook (Excel) icon.

The form the New dialog takes depends, to some extent, on which method you use to launch it. If you invoke it by using the Start menu, you get the full version which incorporates elements from several of the Office modules. You can then choose which type of new document you want to create.

If, on the other hand, you launch the New dialog from within the relevant program, you get a specific, abbreviated form.

Using the full New dialog

First launch the New dialog (see page 11 for how to do this). Then do the following:

1 Activate the relevant tab

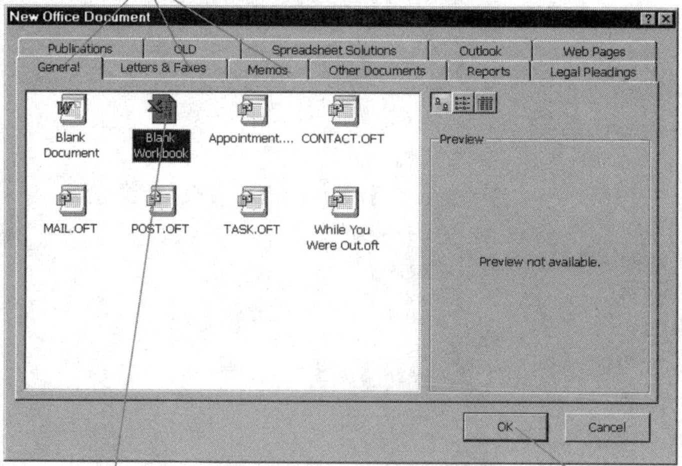

2 Click the template or Wizard you want to use

3 Click here

In the above illustration, a new blank Excel spreadsheet is being created.

Using the New dialog (2)

REMEMBER

The Preview section on the right provides an illustration of what your new document will look like (providing it's based on a template or Wizard).

Using the program-specific New dialog

First launch the New dialog (see page 11). Then do the following:

1 Activate the relevant tab

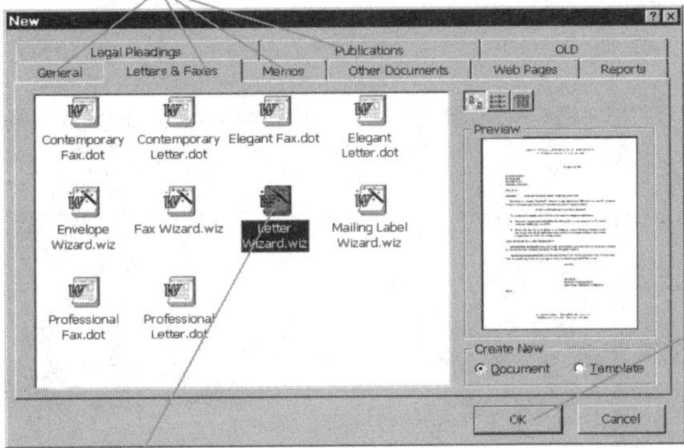

3 Click here

2 Click the blank document, template or Wizard you want to use

In the above illustration, a new Word document is being created, based on the Letter Wizard.

HANDY TIP

See the Handy Tip on page 12 for how to create a new document in Publisher.

Notice that the only new document options you can access in this form of the New dialog are Word-specific.

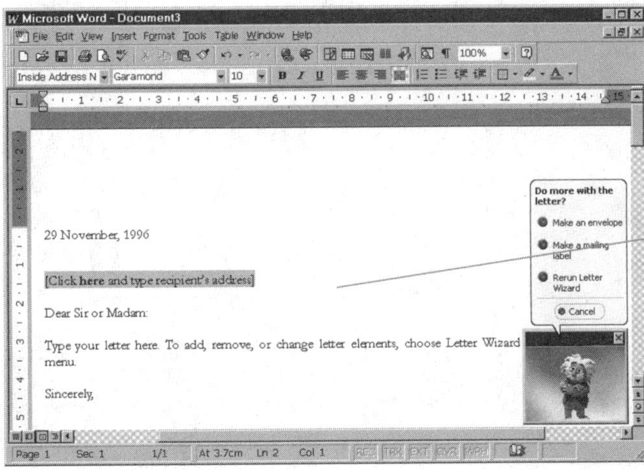

A letter produced by Word's Letter Wizard

Working with templates

If you elected to base your new document on a template, Office creates a detailed document complete with preset text and formatting.

The illustration below shows a new Excel worksheet based on the Invoice template.

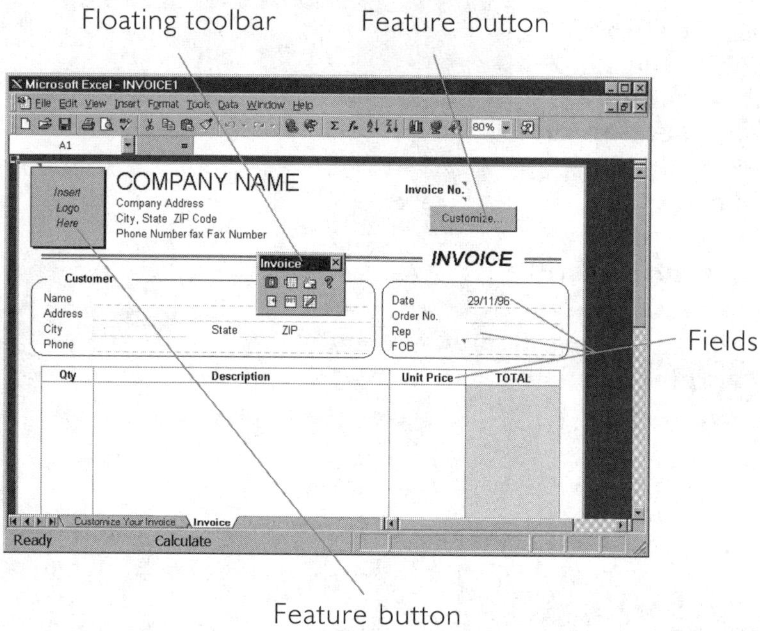

This provides a good idea of how useful and sophisticated Office's templates are. In this case, Office has:

- created numerous predefined fields
- created several additional worksheets
- formatted the worksheet
- inserted special feature buttons which you can click to launch features directly
- launched a dedicated ('floating') toolbar

Amend these as you see fit, then save the template as a document in its own right.

Working with Wizards

You can't use Wizards within Outlook or AutoRoute Express.

When you elect to create a new document with the help of a Wizard, Office launches a succession of dialogs. The illustration below is the first dialog when you run the Word Fax Wizard. Do the following:

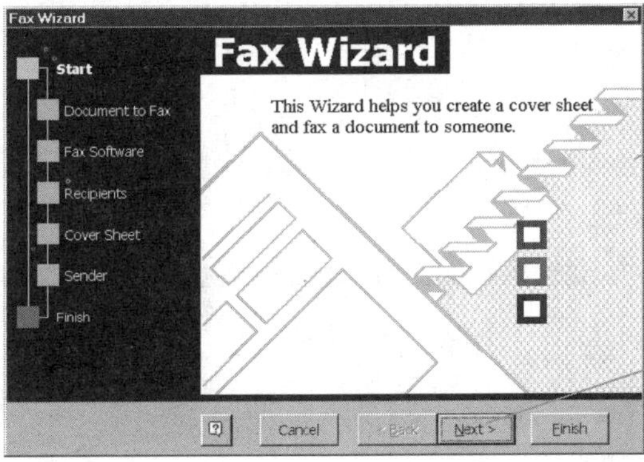

1 Complete the dialog (if appropriate)

2 Click here

Office tells you when you've reached the final dialog by dimming the Next button.

Whichever Wizard you use, in whichever Office module (apart from Outlook and AutoRoute Express), complete the necessary fields and/or click the necessary options. Then click the Next button to move on to the next dialog. Continue doing this until you reach the final dialog. Then do the following:

See the 'Publishing to the Internet' topic later for how to use the Web Page Wizard in Word.

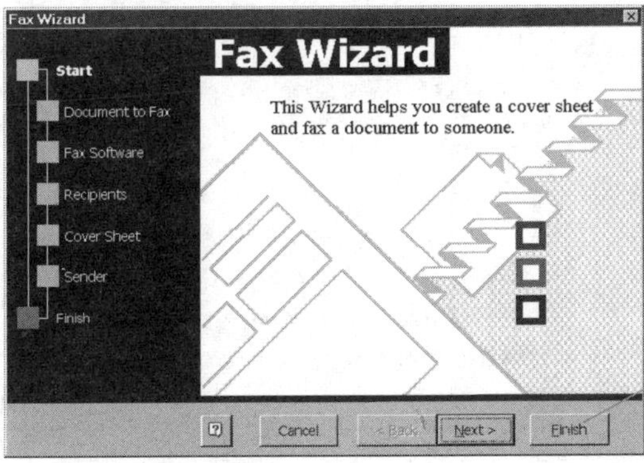

3 Click here

The end result of using a Wizard is the same as using a template: a feature-rich document which you can amend as necessary.

Opening Office documents

HANDY TIP

For how to open an existing schedule or contact/task list in Outlook, see Chapter Six.

HANDY TIP

For how to open a previously defined and saved route in AutoRoute Express, see Chapter Five.

REMEMBER

In Publisher, clicking Open Existing Publication produces the Open Publication dialog. This is slightly different to the Open dialog.

We saw earlier that Office lets you create new documents in various ways. You can also open Word, Excel and Publisher documents you've already created.

In Word or Excel, pull down the File menu and click Open. (In Publisher, click Open Existing Publication in the File menu.) Now do the following:

3 Click here. In the drop-down list, click the drive that hosts the document

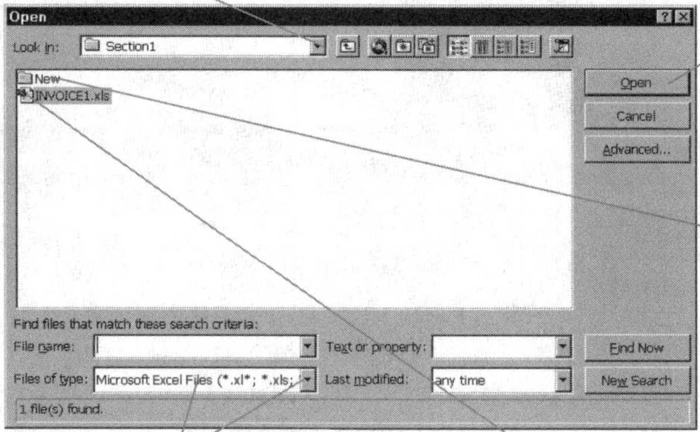

6 Click here

4 If the file is in a folder, double-click it

1 Make sure the correct file type (e.g. 'Microsoft Excel Files') is shown. If it isn't, click the arrow.

5 Click the file

2 Click a file type

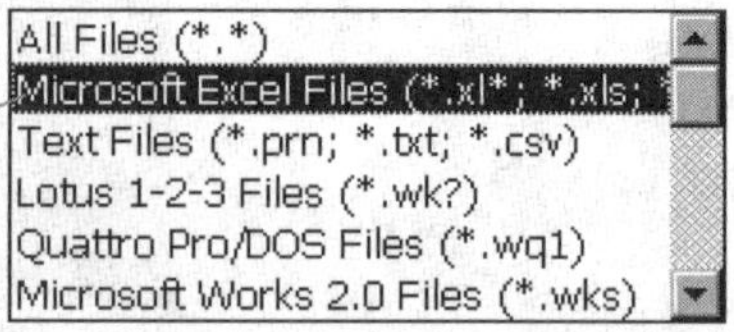

Opening Internet documents

To open Internet documents, you must have access to the Internet (e.g. via a service provider), and you must have installed a modem. Additionally, your connection must be open when you carry out the procedures listed here.

(For more information on the Internet in general, read a companion volume: 'Internet UK in easy steps'.)

In Word and Excel, you can open documents stored at any HTTP site on the World Wide Web.

If the Web toolbar isn't currently on-screen, move the mouse pointer over any existing toolbar and right-click. In the menu which appears, click Web. Now do the following:

1 Click here

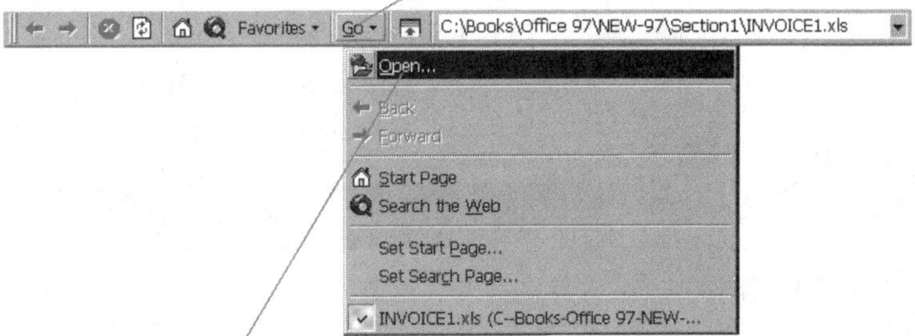

2 Click here

3 Type in a Web address

4 Click here

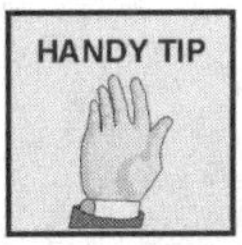

If you don't know the site address, don't follow step 3. Instead, click Browse. Use the Browse dialog (a variant of the Open dialog discussed on page 16) to locate it. Click Open. Then follow step 4.

Saving Office documents

HANDY TIP **See Chapter Five for how to save defined routes in AutoRoute Express.**

It's important to save your work at frequent intervals, in order to avoid data loss in the event of a hardware fault or power interruption. With the exception of Outlook and AutoRoute Express, Office uses a consistent approach to saving.

Saving a document for the first time

In Word, Excel or Publisher, pull down the File menu and click Save (or press Ctrl+S). Now do the following:

REMEMBER **In Publisher, omit step 1. (Additionally, the Save As dialog is slightly different.)**

2 Click here. In the drop-down list, click the drive you want to host the document

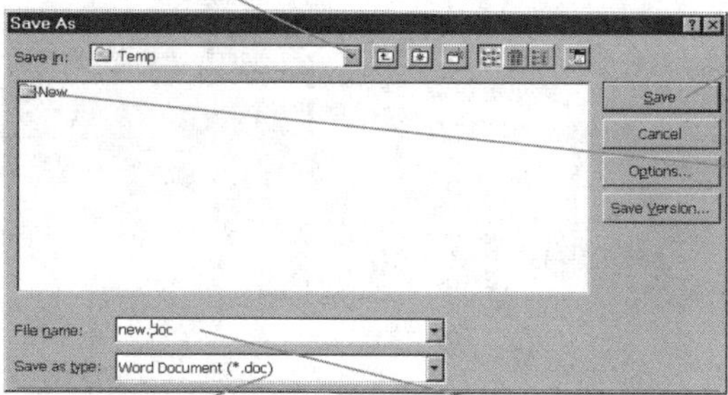

5 Click here

3 Double-click the folder where you want to save the file

1 Click here. In the list, click the format you want to save to

4 Type in a file name

HANDY TIP **A shortcut you can use for either save method: in Word or Excel, click here:**

Saving previously saved documents

In Word, Excel or Publisher, pull down the File menu and click Save (or press Ctrl+S). No dialog launches; instead, Office saves the latest version of your document to disk, overwriting the previous version.

This is Word's Standard toolbar

Saving to the Internet

Re step A – for more information, read a companion volume: 'HTML in easy steps'.

In Word and Excel, you can save documents to any HTTP site on the World Wide Web. This is a two-stage process:

A. saving your completed Office document in HTML (HyperText Markup Language) format

B. copying the HTML files to your service provider

Step A is outside the scope of this book.

Pull down the File menu and click Save as HTML. What happens now differs according to the module you're using.

Word

Word launches the Save As HTML dialog. Complete this as per steps 2-5 on page 18. After step 5, Word reopens the document in HTML format. Note that some of the formatting may have disappeared or may have been changed – the Web supports fewer formatting variables.

Excel

Excel launches a special Wizard. Do the following:

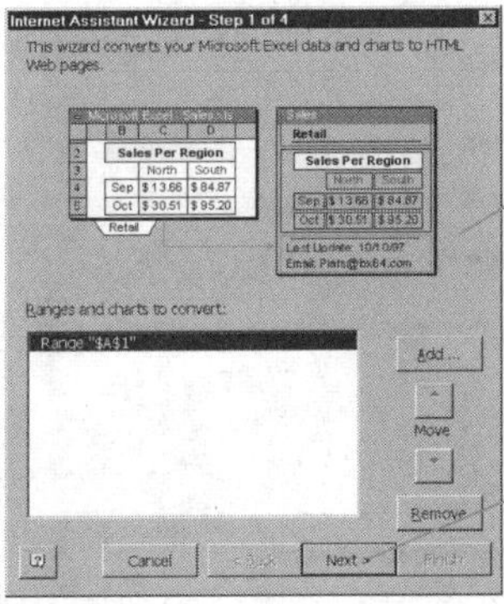

1 Complete the dialog (if appropriate)

2 Click here

For how to save Publisher files to the Internet, see Chapter Four.

Now complete the additional Wizard dialogs which appear. Finally, do the following:

Click here

Publishing to the Internet

On page 19, we discussed how to save an existing Office document in HTML format (for future transmission to the Web). However, in Word you can also use another method to produce documents on the Web. You can run the Web Page Wizard to create a *new* Web document from scratch. (After it's complete, you must still copy the relevant HTML files to your web site.)

In Word, pull down the File menu and click New. Now do the following:

REMEMBER **To publish your completed Word document on the Web, you must have access to the Internet.**

1 Click here

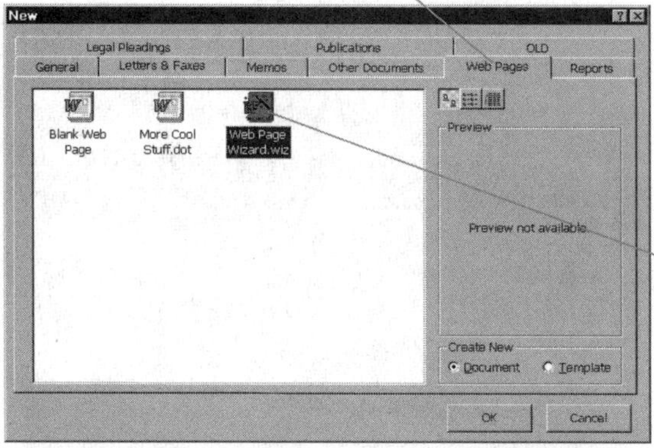

2 Double-click here

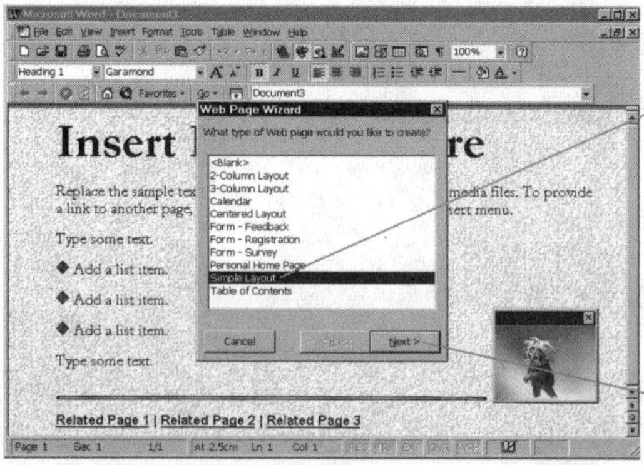

3 Click a layout

4 Click here

Complete the next dialog. Finally, click the Finish button.

Using Office's Help system

To use Contents in AutoRoute Express, click Contents in the Help menu. Now click a relevant topic:

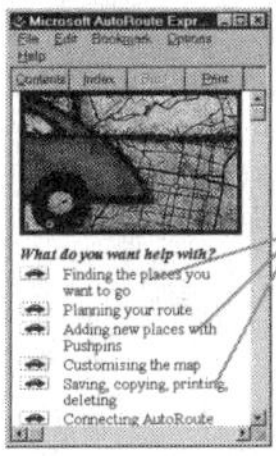

Topics

Repeat until you find the correct Help instructions.

To use Index in AutoRoute Express, click 'Search for' in the Help menu. Do the following:

A Type in a search topic

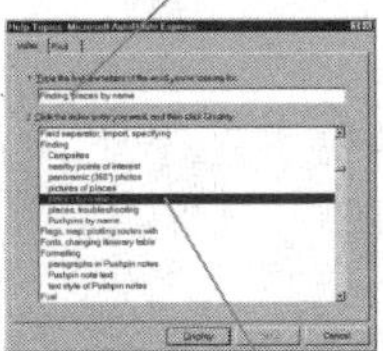

B Double-click a sub-topic

Word, Excel and Outlook support the standard Windows Help system. For instance:

- Moving the mouse pointer over toolbar buttons produces an explanatory Help bubble (see the magnified view below):

These Help bubbles are called 'ToolTips'

- Moving the mouse pointer over fields in dialogs, commands or screen areas and right-clicking produces a context-specific help box. Carry out the following procedure to activate this.

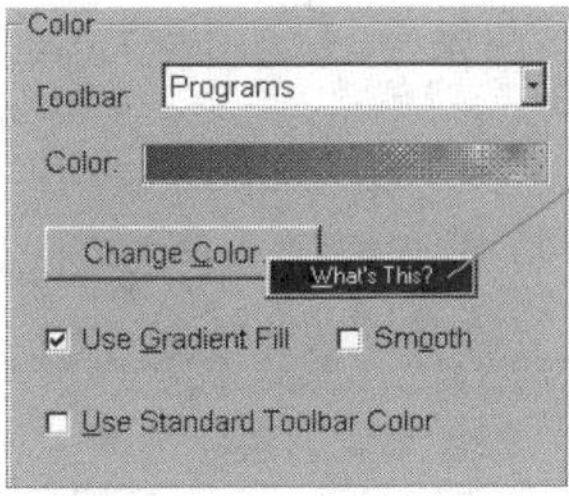

Left-click here for the specific help topic

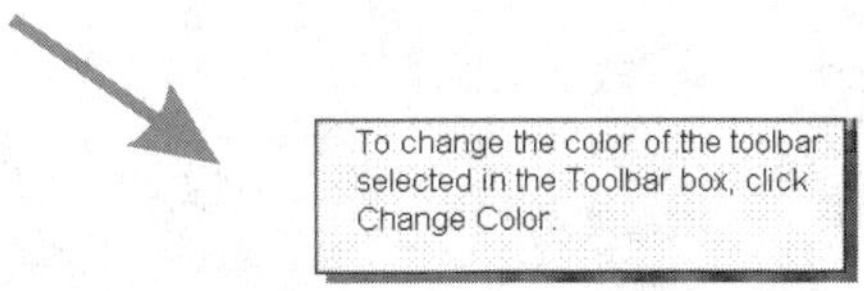

Other standard Windows Help features (e.g. Contents and Index) are also present; see your Windows documentation for how to use these. However, AutoRoute Express and Publisher implement these in different ways – see the tips on the left for AutoRoute's implementation and page 22 for Publisher's.

Office has one further unique Help feature: the Office Assistant – see pages 23-26.

Using Help in Publisher

To close Contents at any time, click this button:

in the bottom right-hand corner of the screen.

Re step A – when you've reached the correct topic, do the following for more information:

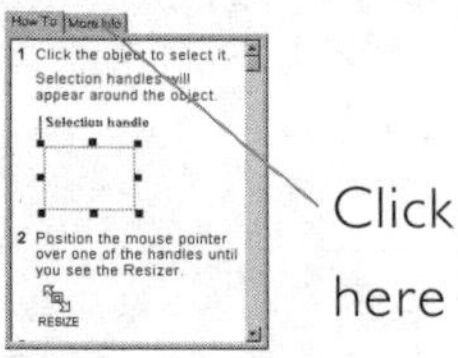

After step 2, follow step A above.

Sometimes, however, Publisher launches a separate window. Do the following after use:

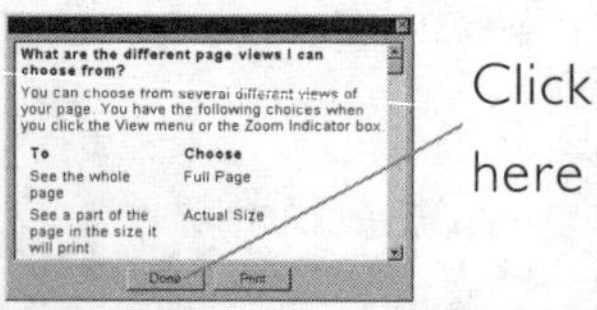

Publisher's Help system is somewhat different.

Using Contents in Publisher

Pull down the Help menu and click Microsoft Publisher Help Topics. Publisher launches a special, context-sensitive screen. Follow step A:

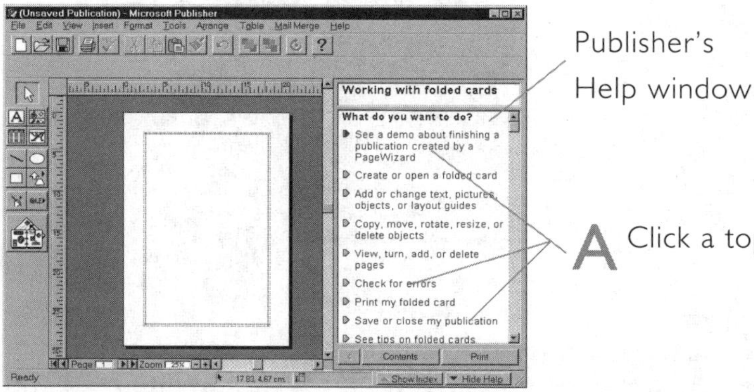

Repeat step A until Publisher displays the correct topic.

Using Index in Publisher

Pull down the Help menu and click Show Index. Do the following:

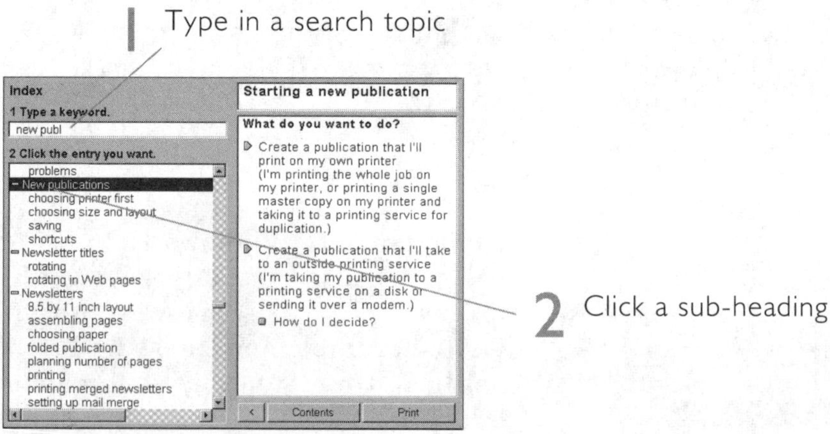

To close the Index at any time, press Esc.

The Office Assistant (1)

Office has a unique Help feature, designed to make it much easier to become productive: the Office Assistant. The Assistant:

- answers questions directly. This is an especially useful feature for the reason that, normally when you invoke a program's Help system, you know more or less the question you want to ask, or the topic on which you need information. If neither of these is true, however, Office Assistant responds to plain English questions and provides a choice of answers. For example, responses produced by entering 'What are ToolTips?' include:
  - Show or hide shortcut keys in ToolTips
  - Show or hide toolbar ScreenTips
  - Turn ScreenTips off
- provides context-sensitive tips
- offers Help which relates to the Office module being used

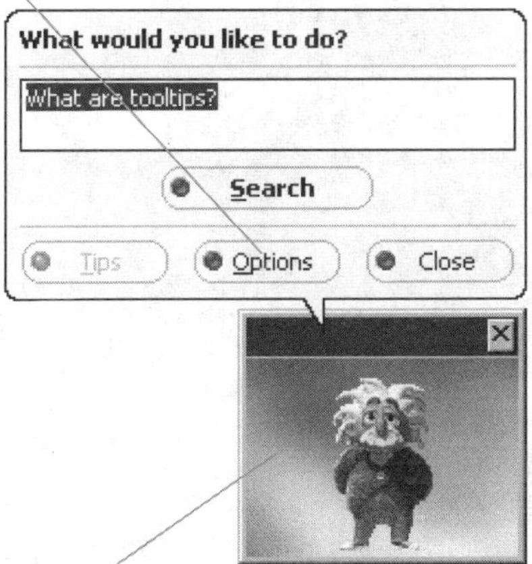

One incarnation of the Word Office Assistant, after it has just launched

REMEMBER

The Office Assistant is not available in Publisher and AutoRoute Express.

HANDY TIP

The Office Assistant is animated. It can also change shape! To do this, click the Options button:
In the dialog which appears, activate the Gallery tab. Click the Next button until the Assistant you want is displayed. Then click OK.

HANDY TIP

If the Assistant Help bubble isn't displayed, simply click anywhere in the Assistant.

The Office Assistant (2)

HANDY TIP **The Standard toolbar – in Word, Excel and Outlook – is the base from which Office Assistant is launched.**

Launching the Office Assistant

By default, the Office Assistant displays automatically. If it isn't currently on-screen, however, refer to the Standard toolbar and do the following:

Click here

Displaying tips

Ensure the Office Assistant is on-screen. Then do the following:

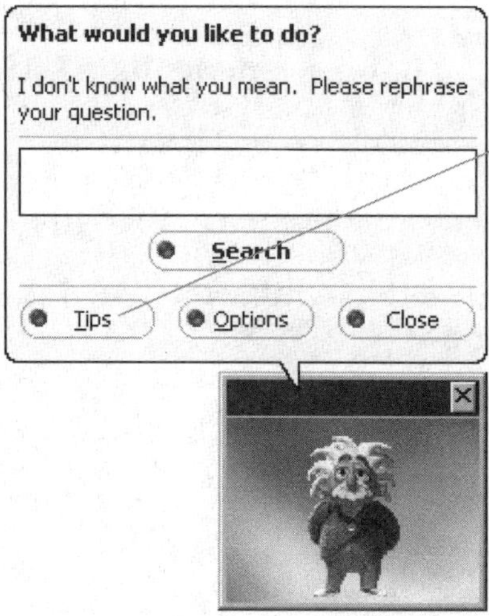

Click here

A context-sensitive tip appears. Do the following when you've finished with it:

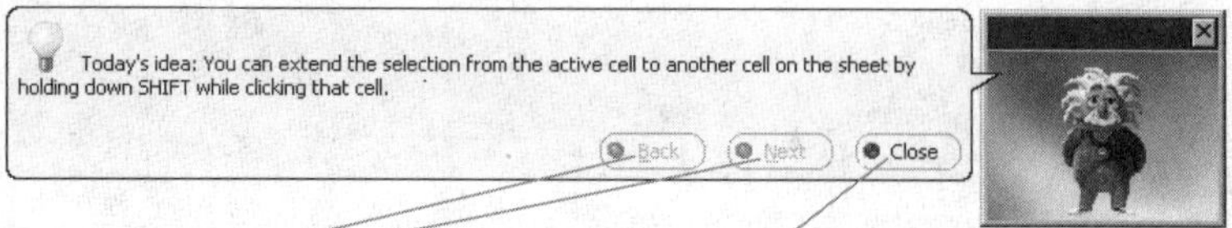

Click here

HANDY TIP **Click Next or Back (if available) to view another tip:**

The Office Assistant (3)

If the Office Assistant isn't on-screen when a tip is launched, the toolbar button which launches it changes to:

The bulb indicates a latent tip

Spontaneous tips

Sometimes, the Office Assistant itself will indicate that it has a tip which may be useful:

Click here to view a suggested tip

Hiding the Office Assistant

If you don't want the Office Assistant to display, right-click over it and do the following:

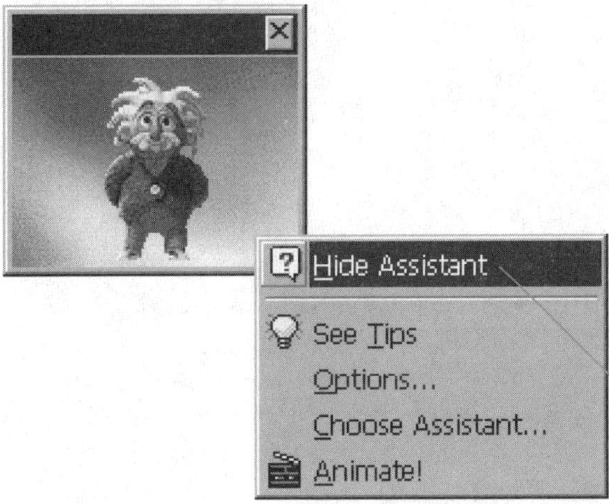

Click here

The Office Assistant (4)

You can use the Office Assistant to answer questions which are expressed in plain English. This is useful when you need to find information on topics which you aren't sure how to classify.

The Office Assistant responds to plain-English questions by displaying a list of topics; you then select whichever one answers your query most effectively.

HANDY TIP

To close an Office Assistant window at any time, press Esc, or click the Close button.

Asking questions

First, ensure the Office Assistant is visible. Then do the following:

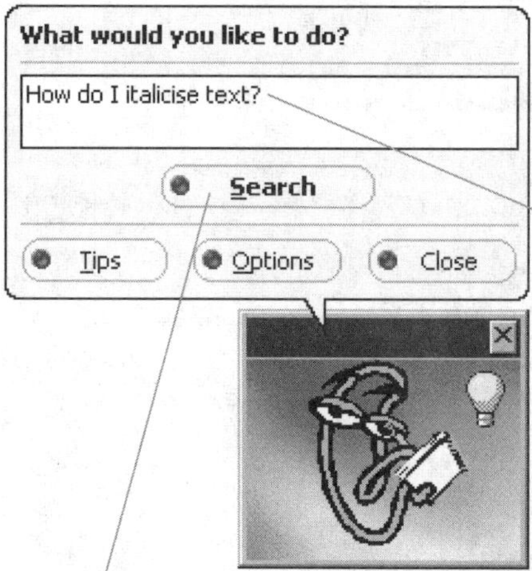

1 Type in your question

2 Click here

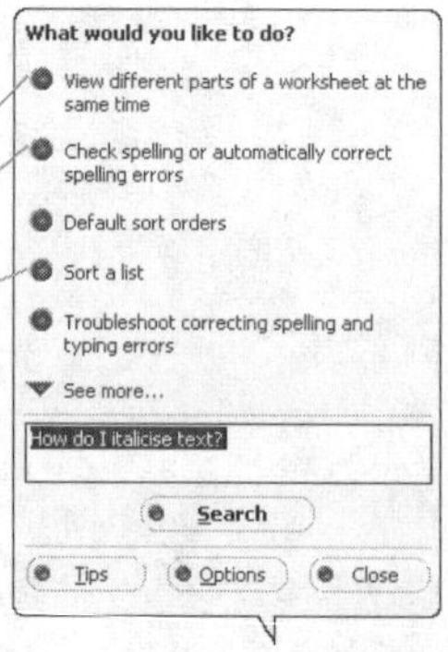

3 Click an option

REMEMBER

Re step 3 – if none of the topics are suitable, click See More. Then click the correct option in the new list.

Chapter Two

Word

This chapter gives you the fundamentals of using Word. You'll learn how to enter text, send e-mail and negotiate the Word screen (using the various views). You'll also discover how to format text and create/apply text styles. Finally, you'll find out how to proof your documents, create automatic summaries, insert/work with pictures and then customise page layout and printing.

Covers

The Word screen

Below is a detailed illustration of the Word screen.

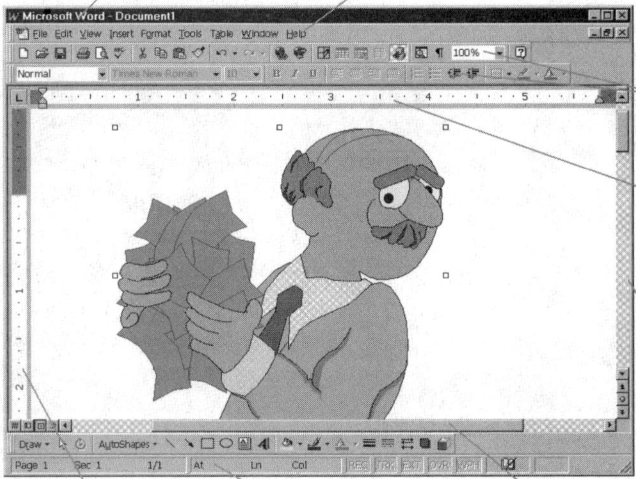

REMEMBER See page 63 for how to import this picture – or many more like it – into Word.

REMEMBER The Status bar displays information relating to the active document (e.g. what page you're on).

Some of these – e.g. the rulers and scroll bars – are standard to just about all programs that run under Windows. Many of them can be hidden, if required.

Specifying which screen components display

Pull down the Tools menu and click Options. Then:

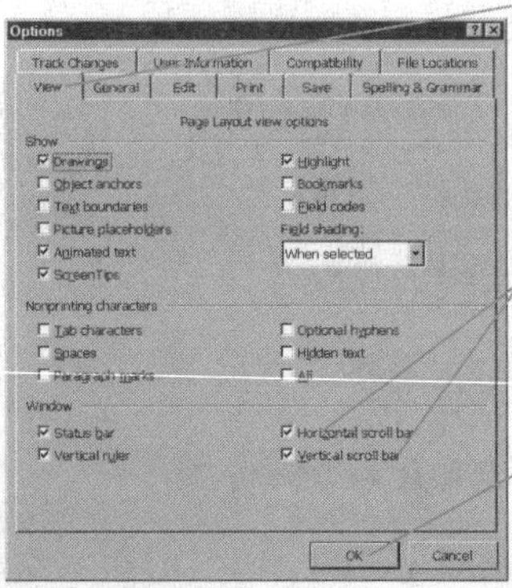

1 Click here

2 Click any option in the Window section to select/deselect it

3 Click here

Entering text

HANDY TIP **You can have Word insert words/ phrases for you.**

Place the insertion point where you want the text inserted. Pull down the Insert menu and click AutoText. In the sub-menu, click a category (e.g. Salutation) then a glossary entry (e.g. Dear Sir or Madam); Word inserts the entry into the active document.

Word lets you enter text immediately after you've started it (it automatically creates a new blank document based on the default template). You enter text at the insertion point:

A magnified view of the Word text-insertion point

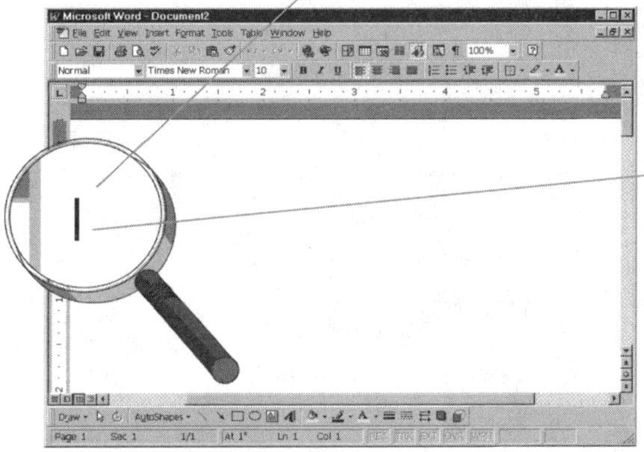

Begin entering text here

Additional characters

Most of the text you need to enter can be typed in directly using the keyboard. However, it's sometimes necessary to enter special characters, e.g. bullets (for instance: ✍) or special symbols like ©.

Pull down the Insert menu and click Symbol. Now do the following:

HANDY TIP **To have Word count the words in the active document, pull down the Tools menu and click Word Count. This is the result:**

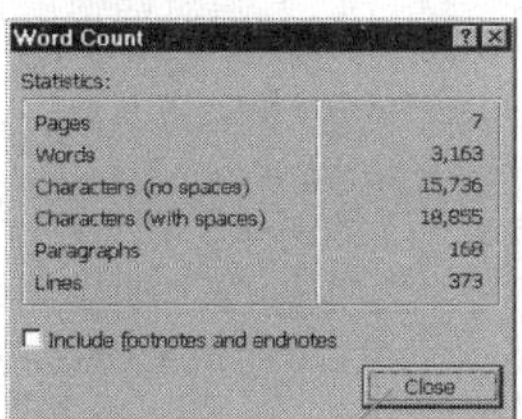

Click here to close this window.

1 Ensure the Symbols tab is active

2 Click here; select the appropriate font from the list

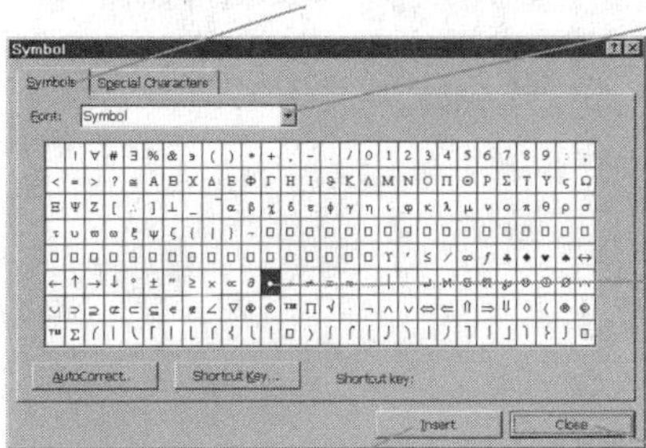

3 Click the symbol you want to insert

4 Click here

5 Click here

Sending e-mail

You can use Word to write and send e-mail messages (provided you've also installed Outlook).

First, compose the document you want to send in the normal way. Then pull down the File menu and click Send to, Mail Recipient. At this point, Office launches Outlook in a special window. Do the following.

3 Click here

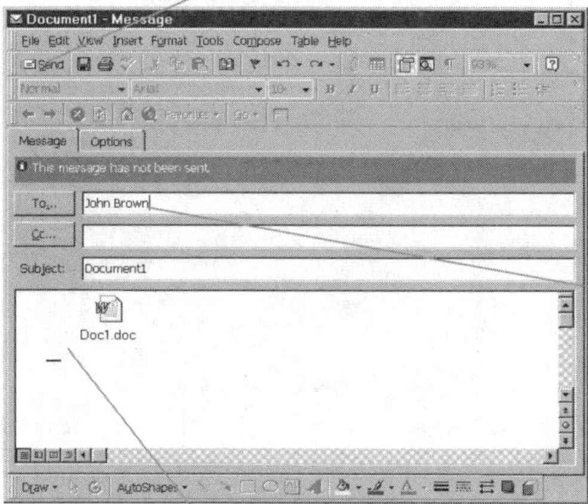

2 Type in the recipient's name

1 Type in a message, if required

If Outlook doesn't recognise the name you inserted in step 2, it launches the next dialog. Carry out step 4 OR 5, then 6:

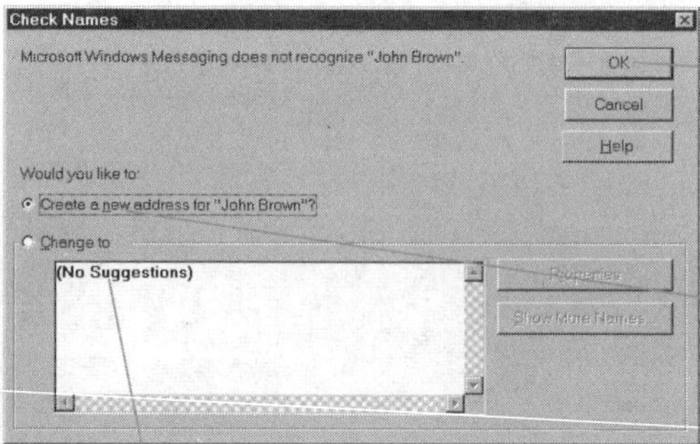

6 Click here

5 Click here to set up a new name/address

4 Click a name/address you've already set up

REMEMBER **You must have specified Word as your e-mail editor. To do this within Outlook, pull down the Tools menu and click Options. Select the E-mail tab, then click Use Microsoft Word as the e-mail editor. Now click OK.**

REMEMBER **To send e-mail, you must have configured Outlook's Remote Mail facility. See Chapter Six.**

REMEMBER **After step 5, a new dialog appears; click OK. Now complete the New Other Address Properties dialog appropriately:**

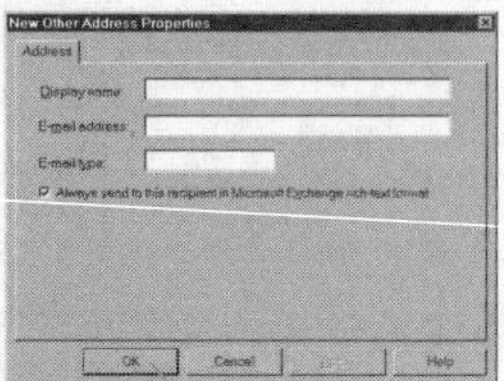

Finally, click OK.

Moving around in documents (1)

HANDY TIP

To move to the location where you last made an amendment, press Shift+F5. You can do this as many as three times in succession.

HANDY TIP

When you drag the box on the vertical scroll bar, Office displays a page indicator (magnified in the illustration) showing which page you're up to.

You can use the following to move through Word documents:

- keystrokes
- the vertical/horizontal scroll bars
- the Go To dialog

Using keystrokes

Word implements the standard Windows direction keys. Use the left, right, up and down cursor keys in the usual way. Additionally, Home, End, Page Up and Page Down work normally.

Using the scroll bars

Use your mouse to perform any of the following actions:

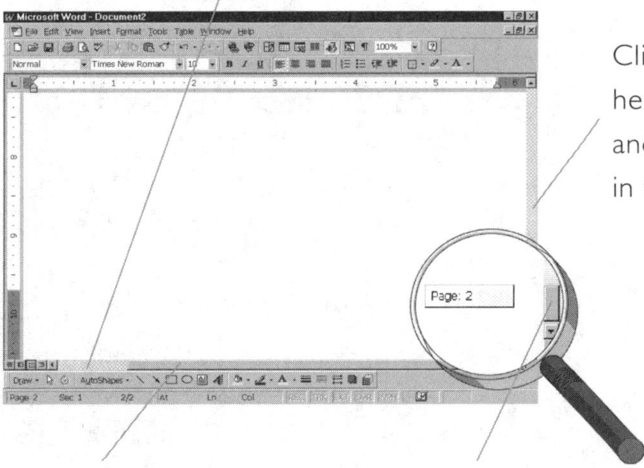

Moving around in documents (2)

Using the Go To dialog

You can use the Go To tab in the Find and Replace dialog to move to a variety of document locations. These include:

- specific pages (probably the most common)
- lines
- pictures

HANDY TIP **You can use a keyboard shortcut to launch the Go To dialog: simply press Ctrl+G.**

Pull down the Edit menu and click Go To. Now do the following:

1 Click the location type you want to go to

3 Click here

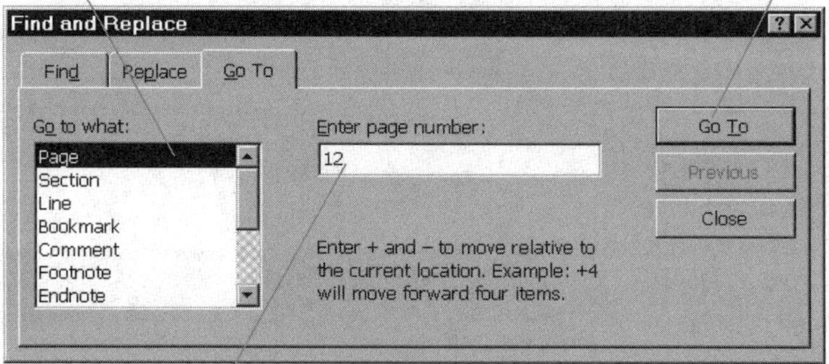

2 Type in the specific location reference (e.g. a number if you selected Page in step 1)

There are some useful refinements:

- You can enter *relative* movements in step 2. For example, if you want to move seventeen pages back from the present location, type in -17. To move five pages forward, type +5...
- To move to the next or previous instance of the specified location (i.e. without specifying a reference), omit step 2. In step 3, the Go To dialog is now slightly different; click Next or Previous, as appropriate. Click Close when you've finished.

Using views (1)

Word lets you examine your work in various ways, according to the approach you need. It calls these document perspectives 'views'. There are four principal views:

Normal

Normal view – the default – is used for basic text editing. In Normal view, text formatting elements are still visible; for instance, coloured, emboldened or italicised text displays faithfully. However, little attempt is made to show document structure or layout (for example, headers/footers and pictures are invisible). For these reasons, Normal view is quick and easy to use. It's suitable for bulk text entry and editing, but is not recommended for use with graphics.

Page Layout

Page Layout view works like Normal view, with one exception: the positioning of items on the page is reproduced accurately. Headers/footers and pictures are visible, and can be edited directly; margins display faithfully.

In Page Layout view, the screen is updated more slowly. Therefore, use it only when your document is nearing completion.

Online Layout

Online Layout is a very useful view. It consists of two panes. In one, text is optimised to make it as legible as possible (the way it displays bears no relation to the way it would print); in the other, Word compiles a summary (an outline view of the document structure called the Document Map). You can click any item in the summary to jump to it automatically.

Full Screen

Unless you have a particularly large monitor, you'll probably find that there are times when your screen is too cluttered. Full Screen view hides all screen components in one operation, thereby making more space available for editing.

Use Full Screen view when you need it, as an adjunct to Normal or Page Layout view.

REMEMBER **There is another view which you'll use frequently: Print Preview. See later in this chapter for more information.**

HANDY TIP **In effect, Word provides another way to view a document: you can 'summarise' it. Pull down the Tools menu and click AutoSummarize. In the dialog, click a summary type and size. Then click OK.**

HANDY TIP **When Full Screen view is active, you lose access to toolbars and scroll bars. However, you can still access the menus by using the keyboard (e.g. Alt+F to launch the File menu).**

Using views (2)

HANDY TIP

To switch to another view, pull down the View menu. Click Normal, Page Layout or Online Layout as appropriate (the view which is currently active has a bullet against it).

The following illustrate the available views:

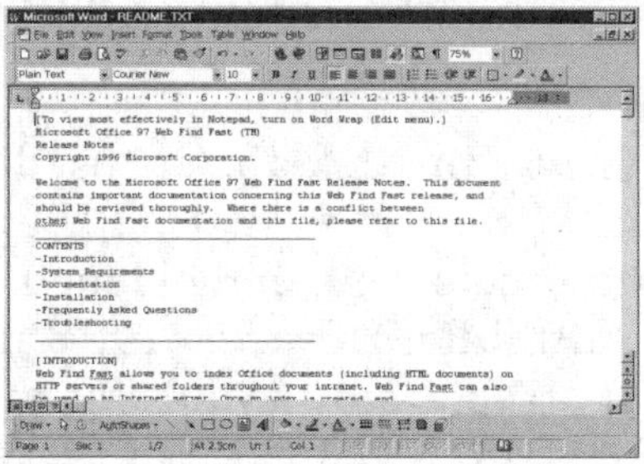

Normal view

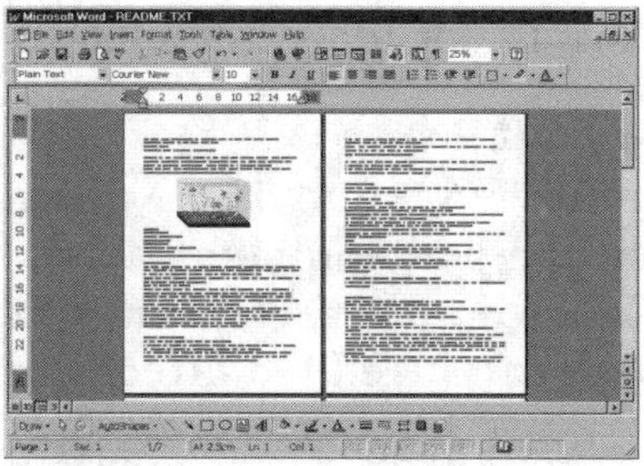

Page Layout view

HANDY TIP

Click a topic in the Document Map: to jump to that section of the open document.

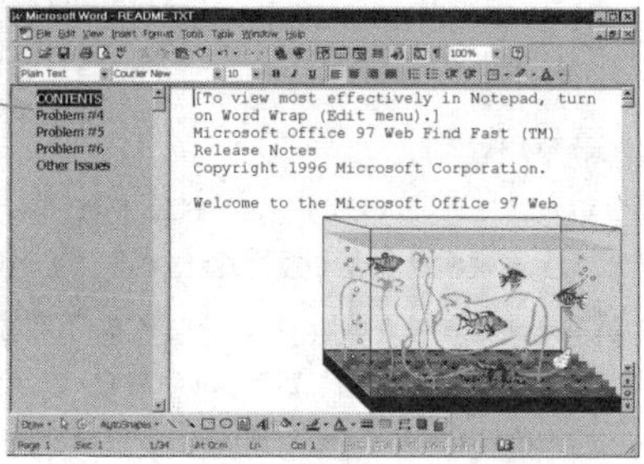

Online Layout view

HANDY TIP

To switch to Full Screen view, pull down the View menu and click Full Screen.
To leave Full Screen view, press Esc.

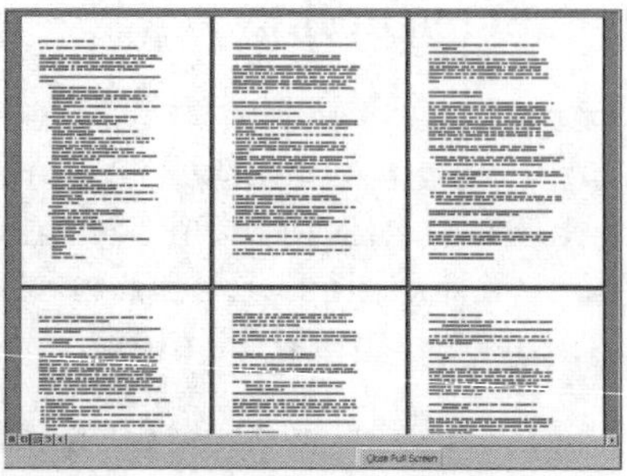

Full Screen (with Page Layout) view

Changing zoom levels

The ability to vary the level of magnification for the active document is often useful. Sometimes, it's helpful to 'zoom out' (i.e. decrease the magnification) so that you can take an overview; at other times, you'll need to 'zoom in' (increase the magnification) to work in greater detail. Word lets you do either of these very easily.

You can do any of the following:

- choose from preset zoom levels (e.g. 100%, 75%)
- specify your own zoom percentage
- choose Many Pages, to view a specific number of pages at once

Setting the zoom level

Pull down the View menu and click Zoom. Now carry out steps 1 & 2 or 3 & 4 (as appropriate) below. Then follow step 5.

The Preview section on the right provides an indication of what the selected view level looks like.

1 Click a preset zoom level

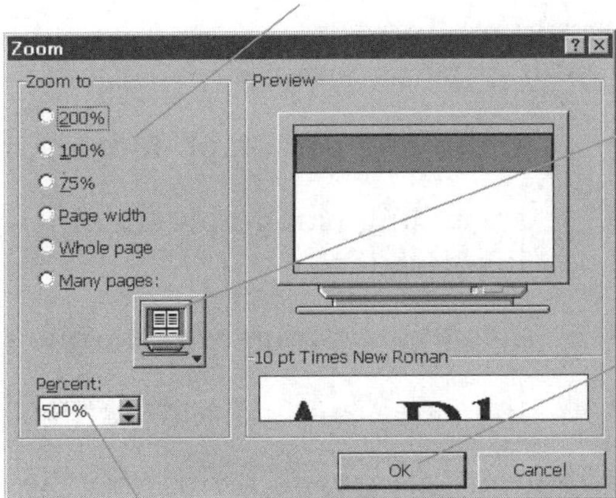

3 Click here

5 Click here

Entries here must lie in the range 10%-500%.

2 Type in your own zoom percentage

4 Click a multiple-page view

Formatting text – an overview

HANDY TIP

You can have Word format the active document automatically.
Pull down the Tools menu and click AutoFormat. In the AutoFormat dialog, click Options. Specify the type of formatting you want applied. Click OK. Back in the AutoFormat dialog, click OK to have Word apply the formatting enhancements.

HANDY TIP

Whenever you type in Internet paths (e.g. 'http://www.microsoft.com') AutoFormat automatically implements them as hypertext links. This means that clicking an address takes you there (if your Internet link is currently open and correctly configured).

Word lets you format text in a variety of ways. Broadly, however, text formatting can be divided into two overall categories:

Character formatting

Character formatting is concerned with altering the *appearance* of selected text. Examples include:

- changing the font and type size
- colouring text
- changing the font style (bold, italic etc.)
- underlining text
- applying font effects (superscript, subscript, small caps etc.)

Character formatting is a misnomer in one sense: it can also be applied to whole paragraphs of text.

Paragraph formatting

Paragraph formatting has to do with the structuring and layout of paragraphs of text. Examples include:

- specifying paragraph indents
- specifying paragraph alignment (e.g. left or right justification)
- specifying paragraph and line spacing
- imposing borders and/or fills on paragraphs

The term "paragraph formatting" is also something of a misnomer in that some of these – for instance, line-spacing – can also be applied to the whole of the active document rather than selected paragraphs.

Changing the font or type size

Character formatting can be changed in two ways:

- from within the Font dialog
- (to a lesser extent) by using the Formatting toolbar

HANDY TIP **Word uses standard Windows procedures for text selection.**

Applying a new font or type size (1)

First, select the text whose typeface and/or type size you want to amend. Pull down the Format menu and click Font. Now do the following:

1 Ensure the Font tab is active

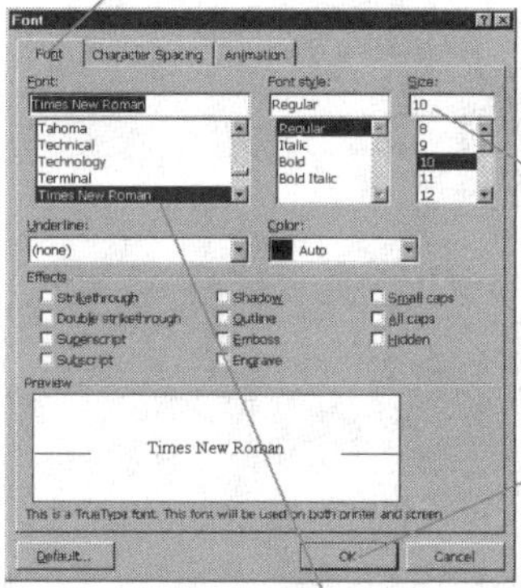

3 Type in the type size you need

4 Click here

2 Click the font you want to use

HANDY TIP **Re step 3 – as well as whole point sizes, you can also enter half-point increments; i.e. Word will accept 10, 10.5 or 11, but not 10.75.**

Applying a new font or type size (2)

Make sure the Formatting toolbar is visible. Now select the text you want to amend and do the following:

Click here; select the font you want to use in the drop-down list

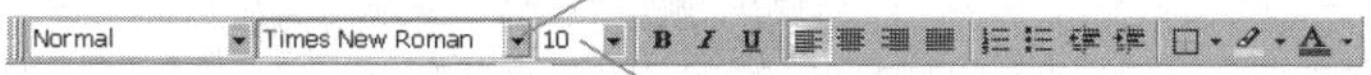

Type in the type size you need and press Enter

HANDY TIP **If the Formatting toolbar isn't currently visible, pull down the View menu and click Toolbars, Formatting.**

Changing text colour

First, select the text you want to alter. Pull down the Format dialog and click Font. Now do the following:

1 Ensure the Font tab is active

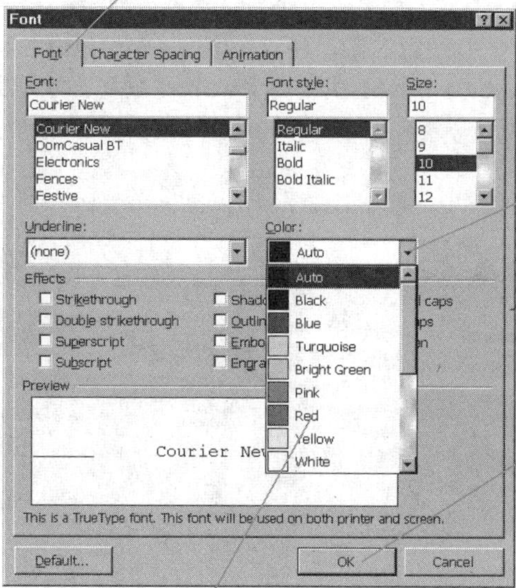

2 Click here

3 Click the colour you want to apply

4 Click here

Re step 3 - clicking Auto sets the colour to black (unless you've amended the default Windows text colour).

Verifying current text formatting

If you're in any doubt about what character/paragraph formatting attributes are associated with text, press Shift+F1. Now click in the text. This is the result:

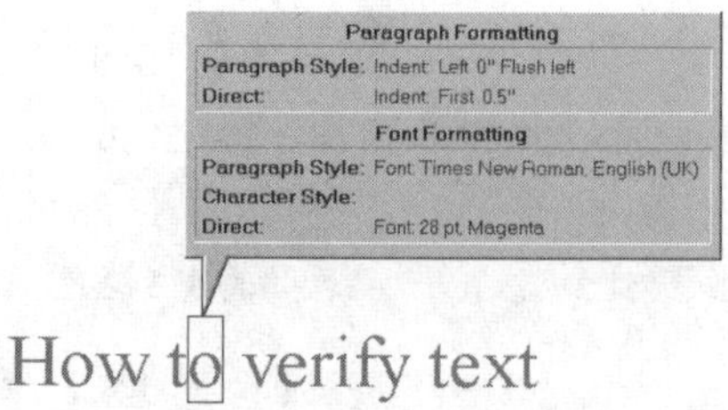

Press Esc to return to normal text editing.

Changing the font style

The default font style is Regular. The additional font styles you can use depend on the typeface. For example, Times New Roman has Bold, Italic and Bold Italic. Arial Rounded MT Bold, on the other hand, merely has Bold and Bold Italic.

You can use the Font dialog or the Formatting toolbar to change font styles.

Amending the font style (1)

First, select the text whose style you want to change. Then pull down the Format menu and click Font. Do the following:

HANDY TIP **To underline text, click here: select an underlining type in the list.**

HANDY TIP **The Preview section provides an indication of what the amendments you make look like.**

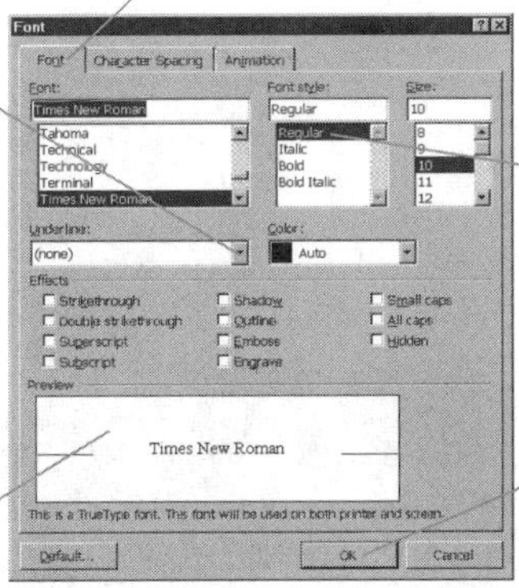

Amending the font style (2)

First, select the relevant text. Ensure the Formatting toolbar is visible. Then do the following:

HANDY TIP **If the Formatting toolbar isn't visible, pull down the View menu and click Toolbars, Formatting.**

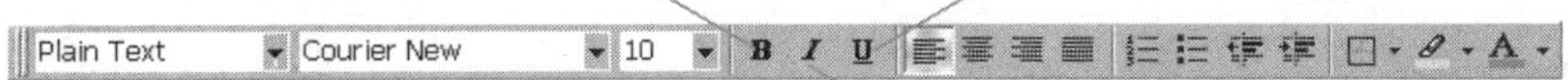

Font effects

The following are the principal font effects:

- *Strikethrough* – e.g. ~~font effect~~
- *Superscript* – e.g. f$^{\text{ont effect}}$
- *Subscript* – e.g. f$_{\text{ont effect}}$
- *All Caps* – e.g. FONT EFFECT
- *Small Caps* – e.g. FONT EFFECT

In addition, you can mark text as hidden, which means that it doesn't display on screen or print.

You can only apply font effects from within the Font dialog.

HANDY TIP

You can also use the following keyboard shortcuts:

Ctrl++	*Superscript*
Ctrl+=	*Subscript*
Ctrl+Shift+K	*Small Caps*
Ctrl+Shift+A	*All Caps*
Ctrl+Shift+H	*Hidden*

Applying font effects

First, select the relevant text. Pull down the Format dialog and click Font. Then carry out the following steps:

1 Ensure the Font tab is active

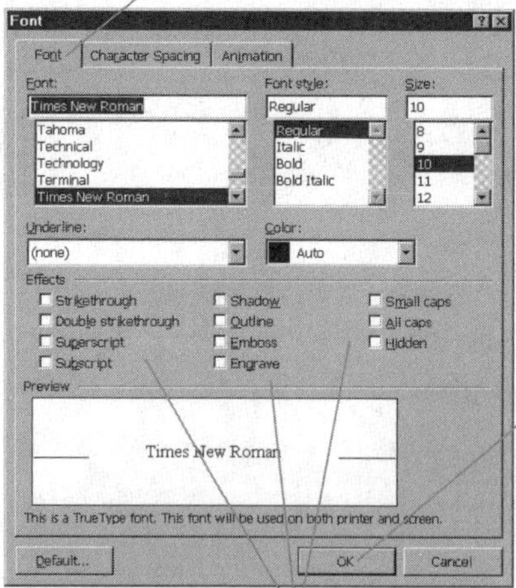

3 Click here

2 Click the relevant option(s)

HANDY TIP

Many of the font effects can be combined – e.g. Superscript with Small Caps. However, Small Caps and All Caps are mutually exclusive.

Indenting paragraphs – an overview

You can achieve a similar effect by using tabs. However, indents are easier to apply (and amend subsequently).

Don't confuse indents with page margins. Margins are the gap between the edge of the page and the text area; indents define the distance between the margins and text.

Indents are a crucial component of document layout. For instance, in most document types indenting the first line of paragraphs (i.e. moving it inwards away from the left page margin) makes the text much more legible.

Other document types – e.g. bibliographies – can use the following:

- negative indents (where the direction of indent is towards and beyond the left margin)
- hanging indents (where the first line is unaltered, while subsequent lines are indented)
- full indents (where the entire paragraph is indented away from the left and/or the right margins)

Some of the potential indent combinations are shown in the illustration below:

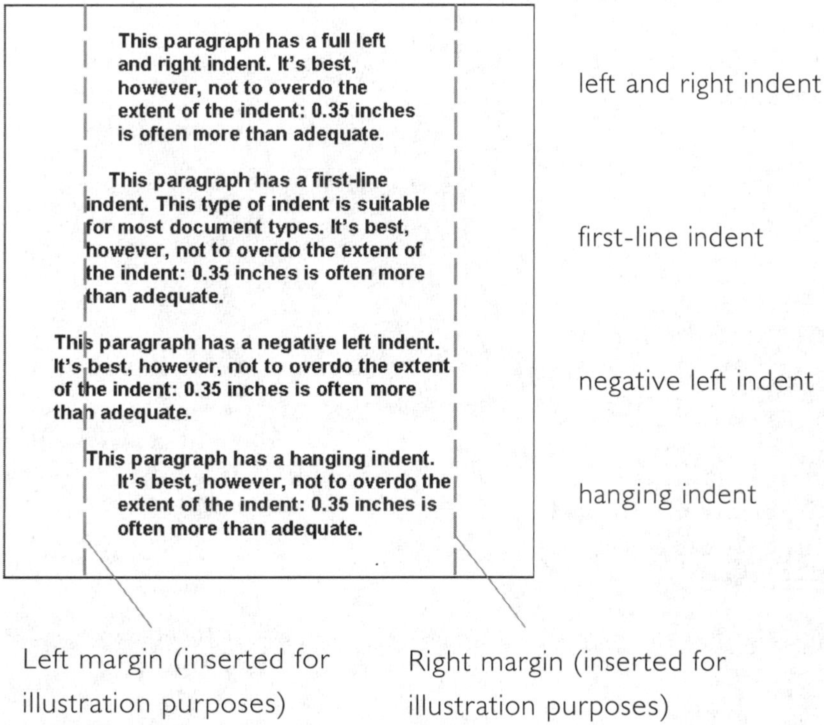

Applying indents to paragraphs

Paragraphs can be indented from within the Paragraph dialog, or (to a lesser extent) by using the Formatting toolbar.

Indenting text (1)

First, select the paragraph you want to indent. Pull down the Format menu and click Paragraph. Now follow step 1 below. If you want a left indent, carry out step 2. For a right indent, follow step 3. To achieve a first-line or hanging indent, follow steps 4 AND 5. Finally, irrespective of the indent type, carry out step 6.

1 Ensure the Indents and Spacing tab is active

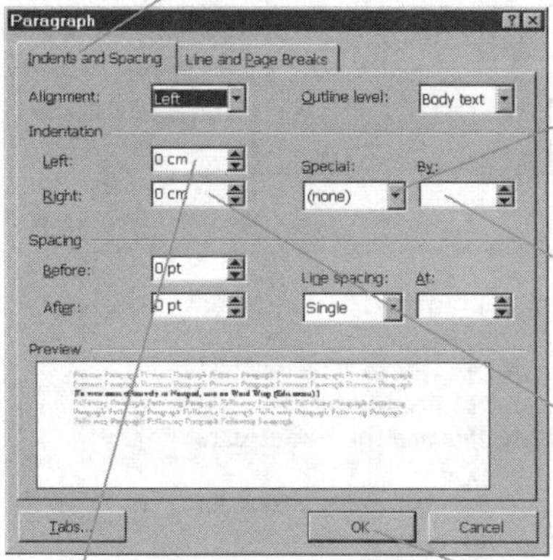

4 Click here; choose First Line or Hanging

5 Type in first-line or hanging indent values

2 Type in the left indent you need

6 Click here

3 Type in the right indent you need

HANDY TIP **Re steps 2 and 3 – type in minus values for negative indents.**

HANDY TIP **If the Formatting toolbar isn't visible, pull down the View menu and click Toolbars, Formatting.**

Indenting text (2)

First, select the relevant paragraph(s). Ensure the Formatting toolbar is visible. Then do the following:

'Jump' to the next tab stop

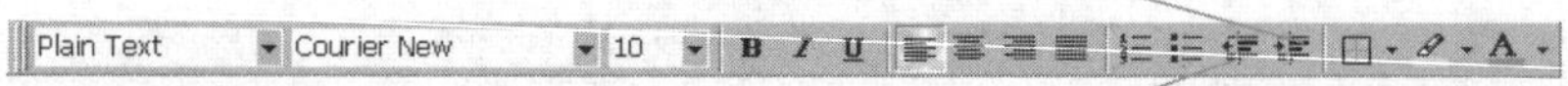

'Jump' to the previous tab stop

Aligning paragraphs

You can adjust alignment from within the Paragraph dialog, or by the use of the Formatting toolbar.

You can only left- or right-align text if the Left and Right Indent values are set to Nil.

If the Formatting toolbar isn't currently visible, pull down the View menu and click Toolbars, Formatting.

Word supports the following types of alignment:

Left alignment
Text is flush with the left page margin.

Right alignment
Text is flush with the right page margin.

Justification
Text is flush with the left *and* right page margins.

Centred
Text is aligned equidistantly between the left and right page margins.

Aligning text (1)
First, select the paragraph you want to indent. Pull down the Format menu and click Paragraph. Now:

1 Ensure the Indents and Spacing tab is active

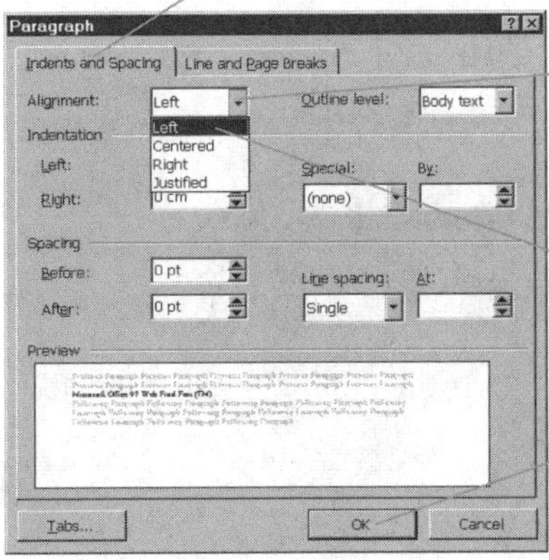

Aligning text (2)
Select the relevant paragraph(s). Then click any of these:

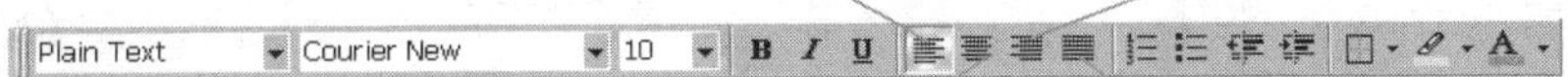

Specifying paragraph spacing

As a general rule, set low paragraph spacing settings: a little goes a long way.

Picas are an alternative measure in typography: one pica is almost equivalent to one-sixth inch. Picas are often used to define line length.

Word lets you customise the vertical space before and/or after specific text paragraphs. This is a useful device for increasing text legibility.

You can only set paragraph spacing from within the Paragraph dialog.

By default, Word defines paragraph spacing (like type sizes) – in point sizes. However, if you want you can enter measurements in different units. To do this, apply any of the following suffixes to values you enter:

- in – for inches, e.g. '2 in'
- cm – for centimetres, e.g. '5 cm'
- pi – for picas, e.g. '14 pi'

Applying paragraph spacing

First, select the paragraph you want to indent. Pull down the Format menu and click Paragraph. Now carry out the steps below:

1 Ensure the Indents and Spacing tab is active

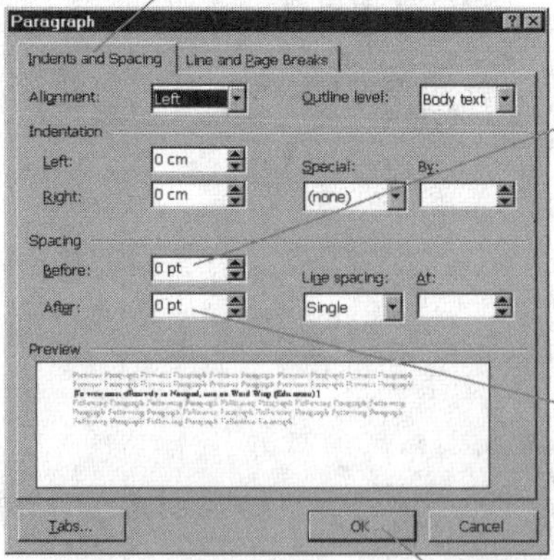

2 Type in a *pre*-paragraph spacing

3 Type in a *post*-paragraph spacing

4 Click here

Line spacing – an overview

It's often necessary to amend line spacing. This is the vertical distance between individual lines of text, or more accurately between the baseline (the imaginary line on which text appears to sit) of one line and the baseline of the previous.

Line spacing is also known as leading (pronounced 'ledding').

Word lets you apply a variety of line spacing settings:

Single

Word separates each line of type by an amount which is slightly more than the type size. For example, if the text is in 12 points, the gap between lines is just over 12 points. Newspapers, particularly, use single line spacing.

This is Word's default.

1.5 Lines

150% of single line spacing.

Double

200% of single line spacing. Manuscripts of all descriptions are nearly always prepared with double line spacing.

At Least

Sets the minimum line height at the value you specify; Word can adjust the line spacing to fit the constituent character sizes.

Exactly

Sets the value you specify as an unvarying line height: Word cannot adjust it.

Multiple

Sets line height as a multiple of single-spaced text. For example, specifying '3.5' here initiates a line height of 3.5 lines.

Adjusting line spacing

First, select the relevant paragraph(s). Then move the mouse pointer over them and right-click. Do the following:

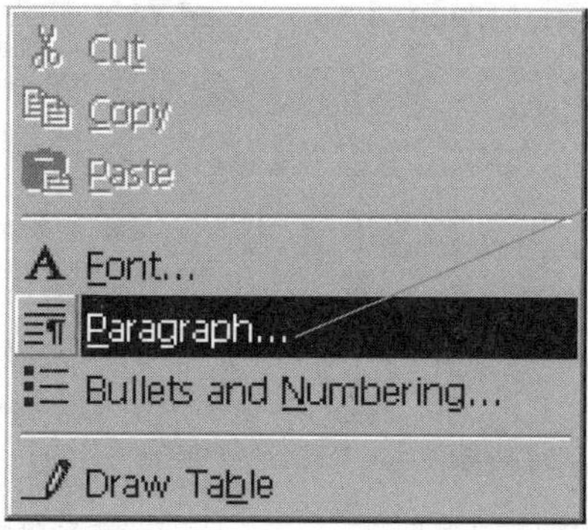

Click here

HANDY TIP **If you've just created a new document, you can set the line spacing *before* you begin to enter text.**

With the insertion point at the start of the document, follow the procedures outlined here.

Now perform step 1 below. If you want to apply a preset spacing, follow step 2. Alternatively, to implement your own spacing carry out steps 3 and 4. Finally, follow step 5:

1 Ensure the Indents and Spacing tab is active

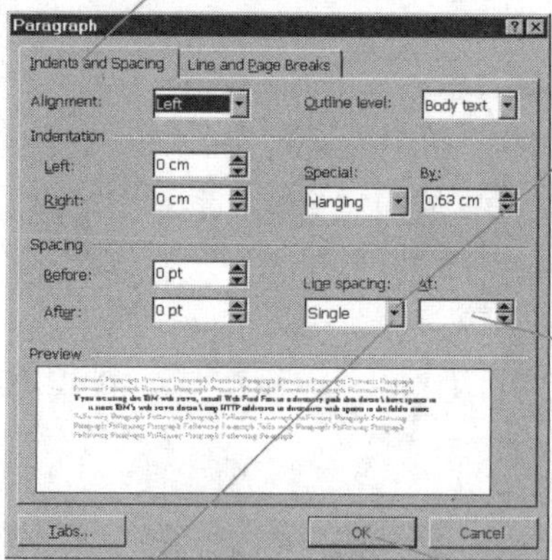

2 Click here; choose Single, 1.5 Lines or Double in the list

3 Click here; choose At Least, Exactly or Multiple in the list

4 If you followed step 3, type in the amount of line spacing

5 Click here

HANDY TIP **You can use these keyboard shortcuts to adjust line spacing:**

Ctrl+1: single spacing
Ctrl+5: 1½ spacing
Ctrl+2: double spacing

Paragraph borders

By default, Word does not border paragraph text. However, you can apply a wide selection of borders if you want. You can specify:

- the type and thickness of the border
- how many sides the border should have
- the border colour
- whether the text is shadowed or in 3-D
- the distance of the border from the text

> HANDY TIP
> **You can also border selected text *within* a paragraph. However, the Borders tab is then slightly different (e.g. you can't deselect the border for specific sides).**

Applying a border

First, select the paragraph(s) you want to border. Then pull down the Format menu and click Borders and Shading. Carry out step 1 below. Now carry out any of steps 2-5 below, as appropriate. Finally, carry out step 6:

> HANDY TIP
> **To set the distance from the border to the enclosed text, click Options. Insert the relevant distances and click OK. Then follow step 6.**

1 Ensure the Borders tab is active

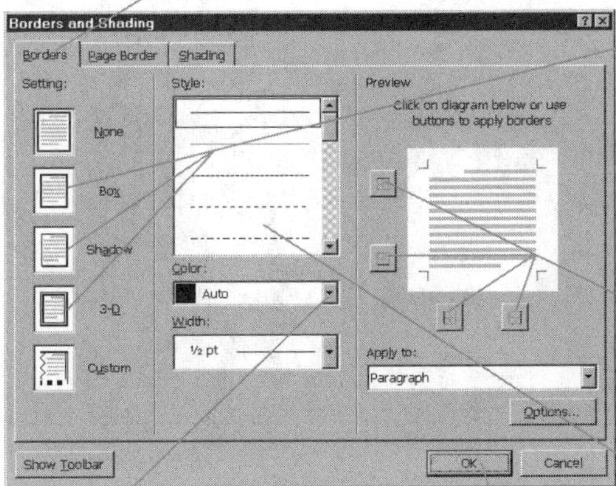

4 Click any of these to border all four sides of the text

5 Click any of the text sides to deselect the border

3 Click here; select the border colour from the drop-down list

6 Click here

2 Click a line type

> HANDY TIP
> **Use step 5 to deselect the top, bottom, left or right paragraph borders. If you want to deselect more than one, repeat step 5 as often as necessary.**

Paragraph fills

By default, Word does not apply a fill to text paragraphs. However, you can do the following if you want:

- specify a percentage fill e.g. 20% (light grey) or 85% (very dark grey)
- apply a simple pattern, if required
- specify a background fill colour
- specify a pattern colour

Applying a fill

First, select the paragraph(s) you want to fill. Then pull down the Format menu and click Borders and Shading. Now carry out step 1 below. Follow steps 2, 3 or 4 as appropriate. Finally, carry out step 5:

1 Ensure the Shading tab is active

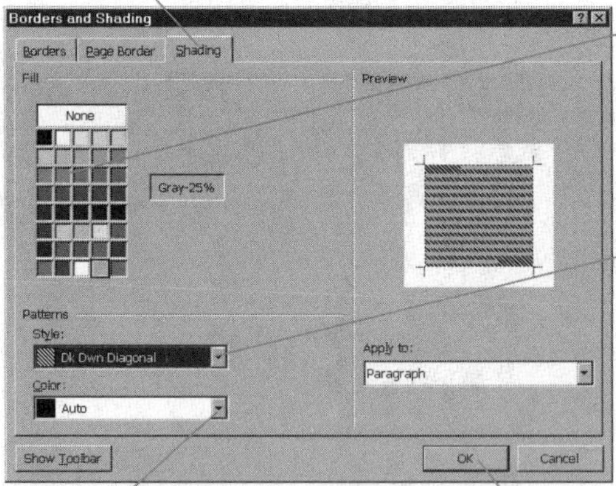

4 Click a background fill colour

2 Click here; select a % fill or pattern from the list

3 Click here; select a pattern colour from the drop-down list

5 Click here

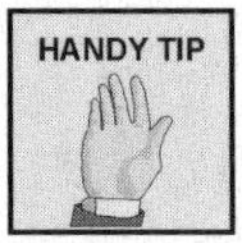

Re steps 3 and 4 – you can achieve unique blends by applying different pattern and background colours. Try reversing the order of these steps, too: this varies the result.

Working with tabs

Tabs are a means of indenting the first line of text paragraphs (you can also use indents for this purpose).

Never use the space bar to indent paragraphs: spaces vary in size according to the typeface and type size applying to specific paragraphs.

When you press the Tab key while the text-insertion point is at the start of a paragraph, the text in the first line jumps to the next tab stop. This is a useful way to increase the legibility of your text. Word lets you set tab stops with great precision.

By default, Word inserts tab stops automatically every half an inch. If you want, you can enter new or revised tab stop positions individually.

Setting tab stops

First, select the paragraph(s) in which you need to set tab stops. Pull down the Format menu and click Tabs. Now carry out step 1 below. If you want to implement a new default tab stop position, follow step 2. If you need to set up individual tab stops, carry out steps 3 AND 4 as often as necessary. Finally, follow step 5 to confirm your changes.

When you've performed steps 3 and 4, the individual tab stop position appears here:

2 Type in the new tab stop default (e.g. 0.35")

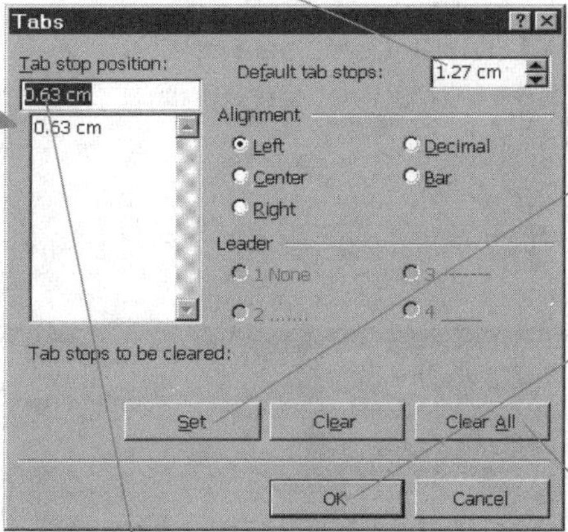

4 Click here

5 Click here

3 Type in a single tab stop position

1 Click here to remove all existing tab stop positions

Searching for text

Word lets you search for specific text within the active document. Even better, however, you can also search for character or paragraph formatting, either separately from the text search or at the same time.

For example, you can if you want have Word locate all instances of the word 'information'. Or you could have it find all italicised words, whatever they are. Similarly, you could have it flag all instances of '*information*'.

You can also:

- limit the search to words which match the case of the text you specify (e.g. if you search for 'Man', Word will not flag 'man' or 'MAN')
- limit the search to whole words (e.g. if you search for 'nation', Word will not flag 'international')
- have Word search for word forms (e.g. if you look for 'began', Word will also stop at 'begin', 'begun' and 'beginning')
- have Word search for homophones (e.g. if you look for 'there', Word will flag 'their')

REMEMBER

Follow step 2 to locate specific formatting. In the extended dialog which launches, click the Format button. Word launches a menu. Do the following:

Click the relevant entry

Complete any dialog which appears in the normal way, then click OK to close it.

Finally, follow step 3 to begin the search.

Initiating a text search

Pull down the Edit menu and click Find. Now do the following:

1 Type in the text you want to find

3 Click here to start the search

2 Click here; in the drop-down dialog, select search options – see the tip

Replacing text

HANDY TIP

Word replaces some words/phrases automatically as you type (e.g. 'accross' becomes 'across'). This is called AutoCorrect.

To add your own substitutions, pull down the Tools menu and click AutoCorrect. In the Replace field in the AutoCorrect dialog, insert the *incorrect* word; in the With field, type in the *correct* version. Click OK.

REMEMBER

When you follow step 3, Word launches a menu; click the relevant entry. Complete any dialog which appears in the normal way, then click OK to close it. Finally, carry out step 5 OR 6, as appropriate.

When you've located text and/or formatting, you can have Word replace it automatically with the text and/or formatting of your choice.

You can customise find-and-replace operations with the same parameters as a simple Find operation. For example, you can have Word find every occurrence of '**information**' and replace it with '*information*', or even '*data*'...

Initiating a find-and-replace operation

First pull down the Edit menu and click Replace. In the Find and Replace dialog, click More. Now follow steps 1 and 2 below. Carry out steps 3 and/or 4, as appropriate. Finally, follow either step 5 or 6:

1 Type in the text you want to find

2 Type in the replacement text

5 Click here to replace the first instance of the specified text

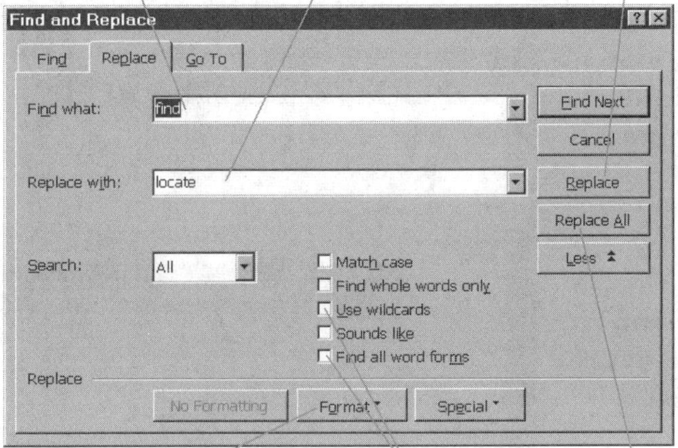

3 Click here to replace formatting

4 Specify the parameters you need

6 Or click here to have Word replace all instances of the specified text

Working with headers

To edit an existing header, simply follow the procedures outlined here; in step 1, however, amend the current header text as necessary.

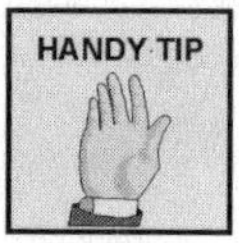

Header text can be formatted in the normal way. For instance, you can apply a new font and/or type size...

You can have Word insert a special code which automatically inserts the page number in the header – see step 3.

You can have Word print text at the top of each page within a document; these are called 'headers'. In the same way, you can have Word print text at the base of each page; these are called 'footers'. Headers and footers are printed within the top and bottom page margins, respectively.

When you create a header, Word automatically switches the active document to Page Layout view and displays the Header and Footer toolbar.

Inserting a header

Move to the start of your document. Pull down the View menu and click Header and Footer. Carry out steps 1-3 below, as appropriate. Finally, perform step 4:

1 Type in the Header text

4 Click here to return to normal document editing

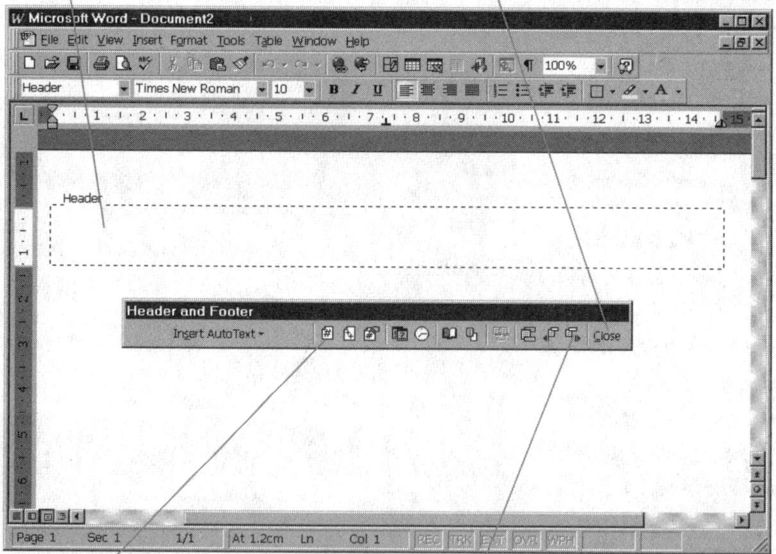

3 Click here to insert a page number code

2 (Optional) Click here to move to the header on the next page

Working with footers

When you create a footer, Word automatically switches the active document to Page Layout view and displays the Header and Footer toolbar.

REMEMBER **To edit an existing footer, simply follow the procedures outlined here; in step 1, however, amend the current footer text as necessary.**

Inserting a footer

Move to the start of your document. Pull down the View menu and click Header and Footer. Word launches the Header and Footer toolbar over the header area. To create a footer, do the following:

Click here

HANDY TIP **Footer text can be formatted in the normal way. For instance, you can apply a new font and/or type size...**

Word moves to the footer area. Now carry out steps 1-3 below, as appropriate. Finally, perform step 4:

3 Click here to insert a page number code

2 (Optional) Click here to move to the footer on the next page

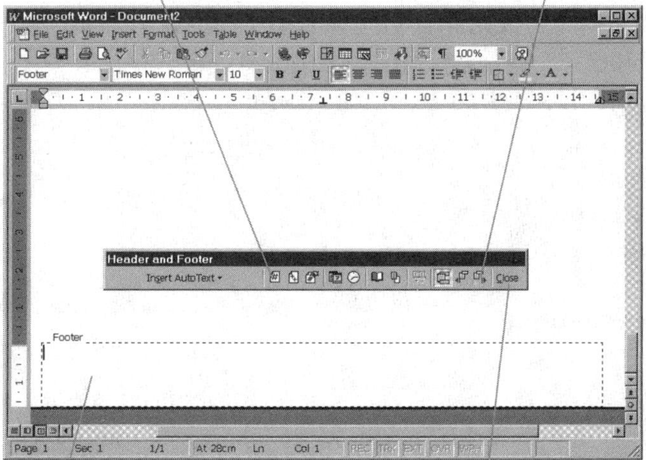

HANDY TIP **You can have Word insert a special code which automatically inserts the page number in the footer – see step 3.**

1 Type in the footer text

4 Click here to return to normal document editing

Undo and Redo

Word lets you reverse – 'undo' – just about any editing operation. If, subsequently, you decide that you do want to proceed with an operation that you've reversed, you can 'redo' it.

You can even undo or redo a series of operations in one go.

You can undo and redo actions in the following ways (in descending order of complexity):

- via the keyboard
- from within the Edit menu
- from within the Standard toolbar

Using the keyboard

Simply press Ctrl+Z to undo an action, or Ctrl+Y to reinstate it.

Using the Edit menu

Pull down the Edit menu and click Undo... or Redo... as appropriate (the ellipses denote the precise nature of the action to be reversed or reinstated).

Using the Standard toolbar

Carry out the following actions:

HANDY TIP

If you select an early operation in the Undo or Redo lists, all later operations are also reversed or reinstated.

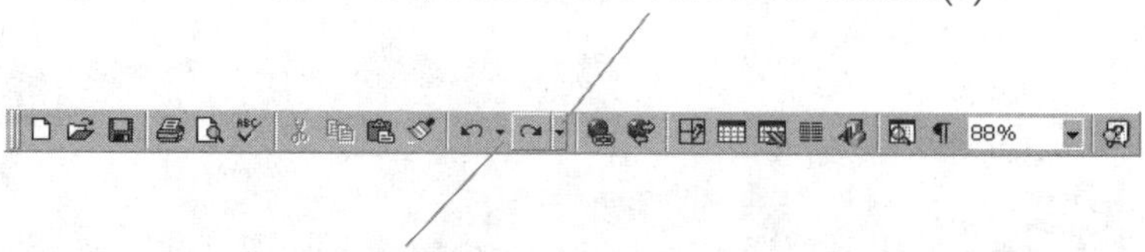

Text styles – an overview

Styles are named collections of associated formatting commands.

The advantage of using styles is that you can apply more than one formatting enhancement to selected text in one go. Once a style is in place, you can change one or more elements of it and have Word apply the amendments automatically throughout the whole of the active document.

Generally, new documents you create in Word are based on a specific template – NORMAL.DOT – and contain the following pre-defined styles as a minimum:

Normal	used for body text
Heading 1	used for headings
Heading 2	used for headings
Heading 3	used for headings

Other templates have many more preset styles.

You can easily create (and apply) your own styles.

Finding out which text style is in force

Word provides a useful shortcut. If you're in any doubt about which style is associated with text, press Shift+F1. Now click in the text. This is the result:

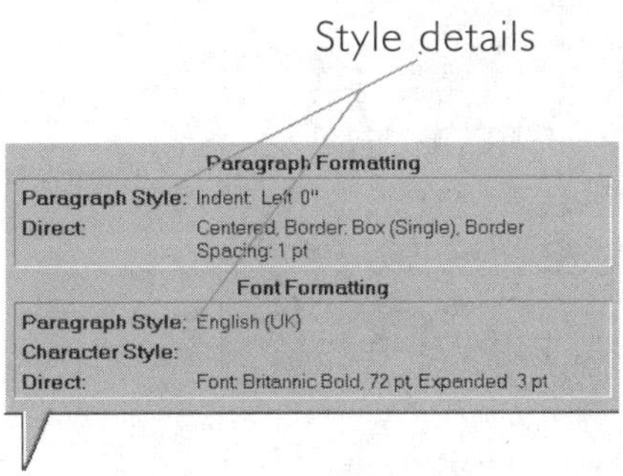

Press Esc to return to normal text editing.

Creating a text style

The easiest way to create a style is to:

1. apply the appropriate formatting enhancements to specific text and then select it
2. tell Word to save this formatting as a style

First, carry out step 1 above. Then pull down the Format menu and click Style. Now do the following:

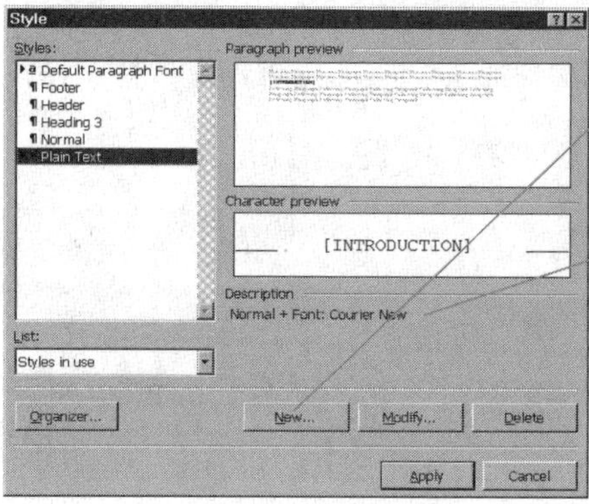

1 Click here

Style details

By default, Word applies the following names to new styles: 'Style 1', 'Style 2' etc.

2 Insert your own name for the new style

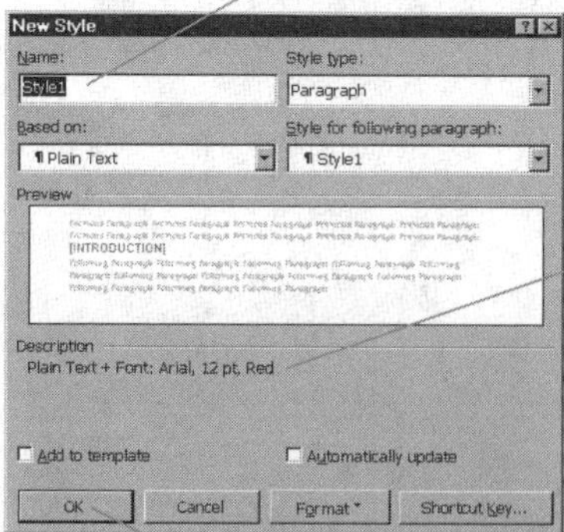

Brief description of formatting associated with the new style

3 Click here

See 'Applying a text style' for how to use your new style.

Applying a text style

Word makes applying styles easy.

First, select the text you want to apply the style to. Or, if you only want to apply it to a single paragraph, place the insertion point inside it. Pull down the Format menu and click Style. Now do the following:

1 Click the style you want to apply

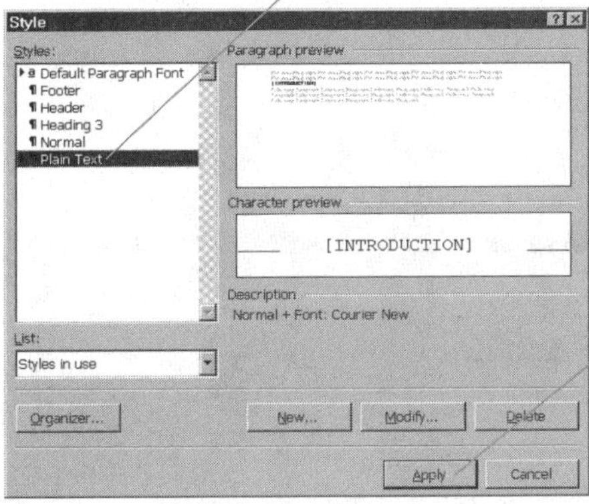

2 Click here

Shortcut for applying styles

Word makes it even easier to apply styles if you currently have the Formatting toolbar on-screen. (If you haven't, pull down the View menu and click Toolbars, Formatting.)

Select the text you want to apply the style to. Then do the following:

1 Click here

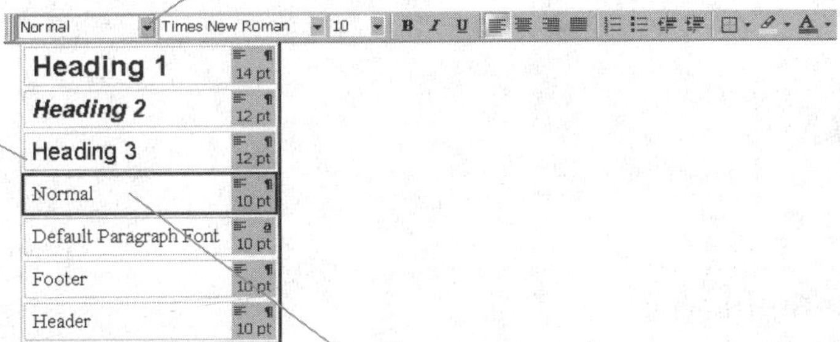

2 Click the style you want to apply

HANDY TIP

Entries in the Style drop-down list display the associated typeface and type size (and most font effects – e.g. italicisation) faithfully.

Amending a text style

The easiest way to modify an existing style is to:

1. apply the appropriate formatting enhancements to specific text and then select it
2. use the Formatting toolbar to tell Word to assign the selected formatting to the style

First, carry out step 1 above. Then do the following:

1 Click here

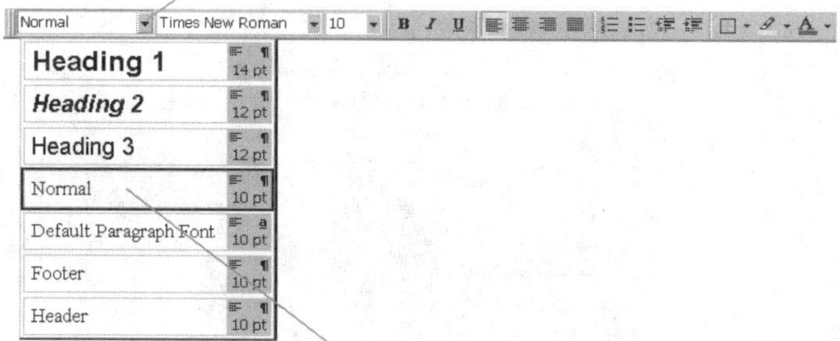

2 Highlight the style you want to modify and press Return

Word launches a special message. Do the following:

1 Make sure this is selected

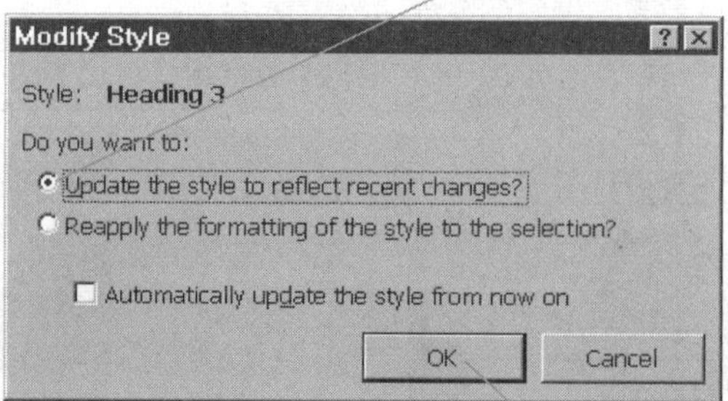

2 Click here to apply the specified amendments to the style

HANDY TIP **If the Formatting toolbar isn't currently visible, pull down the View menu and click Toolbars, Formatting.**

HANDY TIP **You can delete styles, if necessary. Pull down the Format menu and click Style. In the Styles field in the Style dialog, select a style and click Delete. Do the following:**

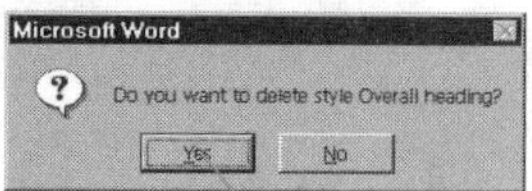

Click here

REMEMBER **When you delete a style, any text associated with it automatically has the Normal style applied to it.**

Spell- and grammar-checking (1)

REMEMBER **Word checks spelling and grammar simultaneously.**

Word lets you check text in two ways:

- on-the-fly, as you type in text
- separately, after the text has been entered

Checking text on-the-fly

This is the default. When automatic checking is in force, Word flags words it doesn't recognise with a red underline (in the case of misspellings) or a green line (for grammatical errors). If the word or phrase is wrong, right-click in it. Then do one of the following:

HANDY TIP **Word includes Smart spelling: it recognises often-used names. These include:**
- **your name**
- **personal and business names**
- **country names**

It also detects typing patterns – for example, if you frequently type HELP (i.e. in capitals), Word will stop flagging it.

Word often provides a list of alternative suggestions. If one is correct, click it; Word replaces the flagged word with the correct version

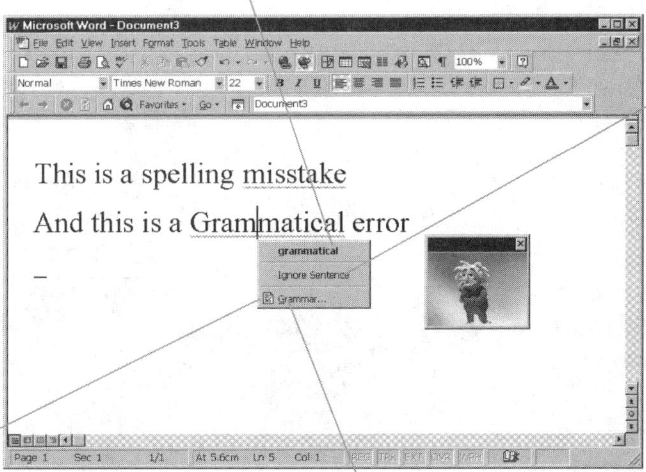

If you want the flagged word or phrase to stand, click here

If the flagged word is wrong but can't be corrected now, click here; complete the dialog which launches (see page 60)

HANDY TIP **Here, we're correcting a grammatical error. If a spelling error has been flagged, this section of the menu shows:**

Disabling on-the-fly checking

Pull down the Tools menu and click Options. Activate the Spelling and Grammar tab, then click 'Check spelling as you type' (the cross disappears) and/or 'Check grammar as you type'. Finally, click OK.

Spell- and grammar-checking (2)

REMEMBER

Word makes use of two separate dictionaries. One – CUSTOM.DIC – can be thought of as yours. When you click the Add button (see the tip below), the flagged word is stored in this and recognised in future checking sessions.

HANDY TIP

If you're correcting a spelling error, you have two further options. Click Add to have the flagged word stored in CUSTOM.DIC. Alternatively, click Change All to have Word substitute its suggestion for *all* future instances of the flagged word (within the current session).

REMEMBER

Word's Office Assistant explains grammatical points here.

Checking text separately

To check all the text within the active document in one go, pull down the Tools menu and click Spelling and Grammar. Word starts spell- and grammar-checking the document from the beginning. When it encounters a word or phrase it doesn't recognise, Word flags it and produces a special dialog (see below). Usually, it provides alternative suggestions; if one of these is correct, you can opt to have it replace the flagged word. You can do this singly (i.e. just this instance is replaced) or globally (where all future instances – within the current checking session – are replaced).

Alternatively, you can have Word ignore *this* instance of the flagged word, ignore *all* future instances of the word or add the word to CUSTOM.DIC (see the tips). After any of these, Word resumes checking.

Carry out step 1 below, then follow step 2. Alternatively, carry out step 3 or 4.

1 If one of the suggestions here is correct, click it, then follow step 2

3 Click here to ignore just this instance

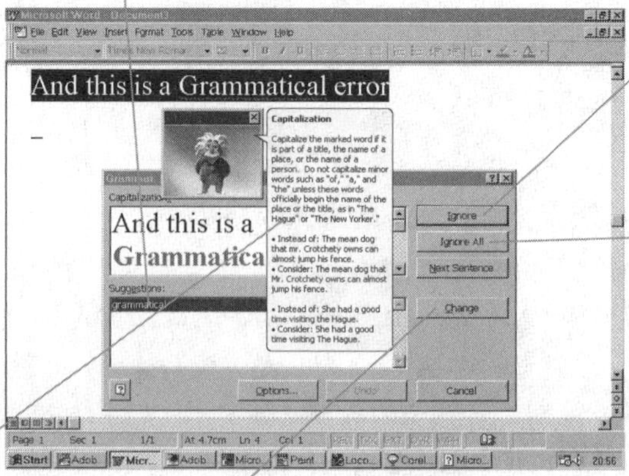

4 Click here to ignore all future instances

2 Click here to replace this instance

Searching for synonyms

Word lets you search for synonyms while you're editing the active document. You do this by calling up Word's resident thesaurus. The thesaurus categorises words into meanings, and each meaning is allocated various synonyms from which you can choose.

As a bonus, the thesaurus also supplies related words, and antonyms. For example, if you look up 'error' in the thesaurus, Word lists 'err' under the heading 'Related Words'.

Using the thesaurus

First, select the word for which you require a synonym or antonym (or simply position the insertion point within it). Pull down the Tools menu and click Language, Thesaurus. Now do the following:

The selected word appears here

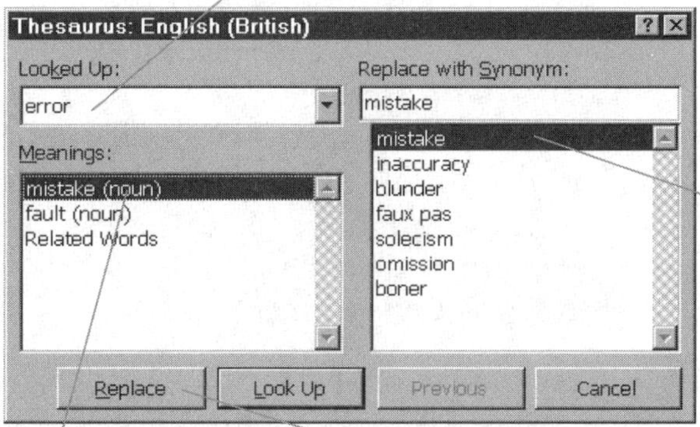

2 Click a replacement synonym or antonym

1 Click the appropriate meaning, or click Antonyms, if appropriate

3 Click here to substitute the synonym or antonym for the selected word

Working with pictures

Word lets you add colour or greyscale pictures to the active document. Pictures – also called graphics – include:

- drawings produced in other programs
- clip art
- scanned photographs

Pictures are stored in various third-party formats. These formats are organised into two basic types:

Bitmap images

Bitmaps consist of pixels (dots) arranged in such a way that they form a graphic image. Because of the very nature of bitmaps, the question of 'resolution' – the sharpness of an image expressed in dpi (dots per inch) – is very important. Bitmaps look best if they're displayed at their correct resolution. Word can manipulate a wide variety of third-party bitmap graphics formats. These include: PCX, TIF, TGA and GIF.

Vector images

You can also insert vector graphics files into Word documents. Vector images consist of and are defined by algebraic equations. They're less complex than bitmaps: they contain less detail. Vector files can also include bitmap information.

Irrespective of the format type, Word can incorporate pictures with the help of special 'filters'. These are special mini-programs whose job it is to translate third-party formats into a form which Word can use. However, several supported formats do not require filters. The two main ones are:

- Windows Bitmap. A popular bitmap format. File suffix: BMP
- Windows Metafile. A frequently used vector format. Used for information exchange between just about all Windows programs. File suffix: WMF

Other examples of vector formats include:

CGM	Computer Graphics Metafile
EPS	Encapsulated PostScript (also includes bitmap data)

Inserting pictures

First, position the insertion point at the location within the active document where you want to insert the picture. Pull down the Insert menu and do the following:

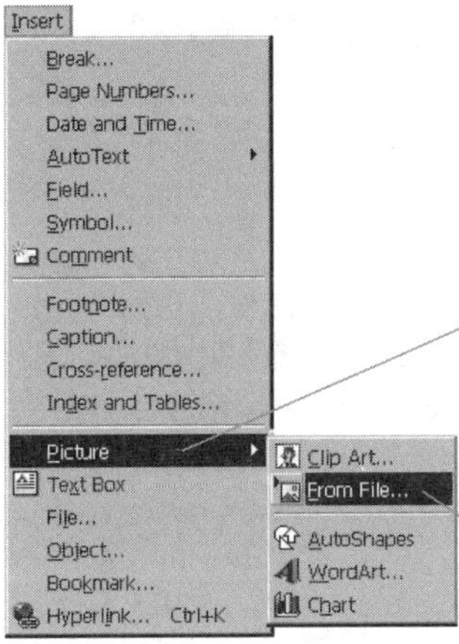

1 Click here

2 Click here

REMEMBER **Word provides a preview of what the picture will look like when it's been imported:**

Now carry out the following steps:

4 Click here. In the drop-down list, click the drive/folder that hosts the picture

6 Click here

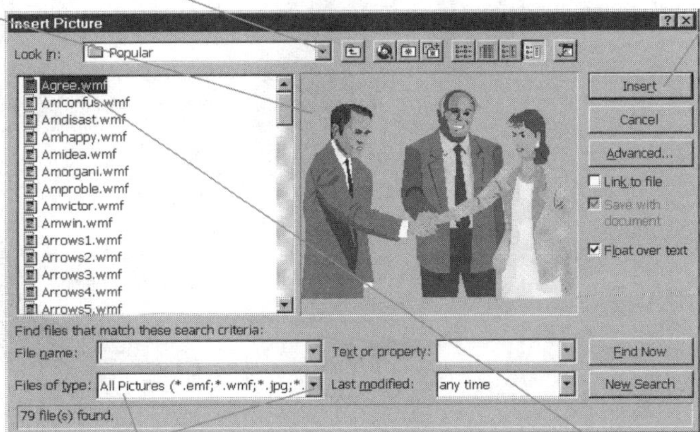

3 Make sure All Pictures is shown. If it isn't, click the arrow and select it from the drop-down list

5 Click the picture file

Editing pictures

Once you've inserted pictures into a Word document, you can amend them in a variety of ways. For instance, you can:

- rescale them
- apply a border
- crop them
- move them

To carry out any of these operations, you have to select the relevant picture first. To do this, simply position the mouse pointer over the image and left-click once. Word surrounds the image with eight handles. These are positioned at the four corners, and midway on each side. The illustration below demonstrates these:

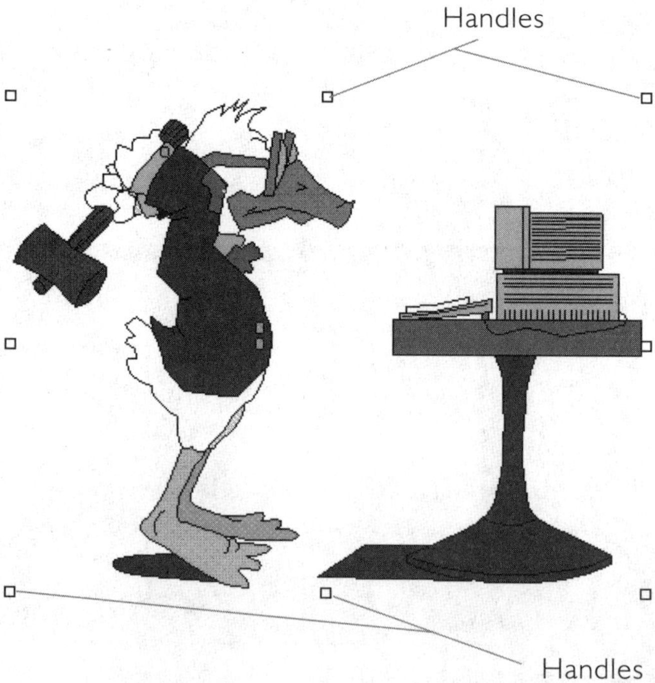

Rescaling pictures

There are two ways in which you can rescale pictures:

- proportionally, where the height/width ratio remains constant
- disproportionately, where the height/width ratio is disrupted (this is sometimes called 'warping' or 'skewing')

To rescale a picture, first select it. Then move the mouse pointer over:

- one of the corner handles, if you want to rescale the image proportionately,

or

- one of the handles in the middle of the sides, if you want to warp it

In either eventuality, the mouse pointer changes to a double-headed arrow. Click and hold down the left mouse button. Drag outwards to increase the image size or inwards to decrease it. Release the mouse button to confirm the change.

Here, the image has been skewed from the right inwards

To move a picture on the page, select it. Then move the mouse pointer over the picture. Click and hold down the left mouse button; drag the image to a new location. Release the mouse button to confirm the move.

To control how text aligns around a picture, select it. Pull down the Format menu and click Picture. In the Format Picture dialog, activate the Wrapping tab. Now select a text wrap option, e.g.:

where text aligns around the top and bottom of the image, but not the sides. Finally, click OK.

Bordering pictures

By default, Word does not apply a border to inserted pictures. However, you can apply a wide selection of borders if you want. You can specify:

- the style and/or thickness of the border
- the border colour
- whether the border is dashed

Applying a border

First, select the picture you want to border. Then pull down the Format menu and click Borders and Shading. Now carry out step 1 below. Perform steps 2-5, as appropriate. Finally, carry out step 6:

1 Ensure the Colors and Lines tab is active

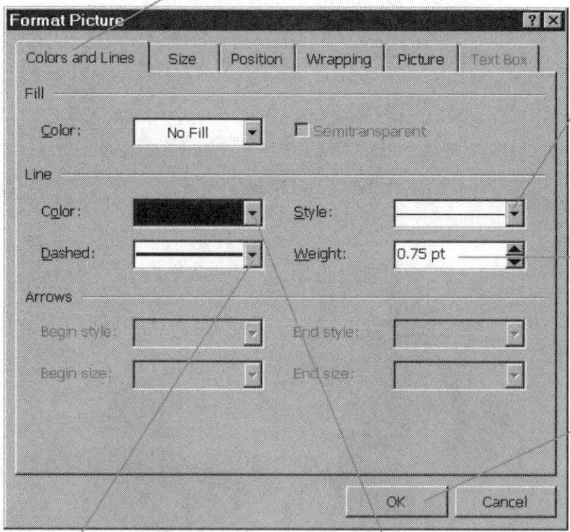

3 Click here; select a style from the list

4 Type in a line weight

6 Click here

5 (Optional) click here; select a dashed pattern from the drop-down list

2 Click here; select the border colour from the drop-down list

Cropping pictures

Cropping is the process of trimming the edges off a picture, either to make it fit within a smaller space or to remove parts that are unwanted.

Cropping a picture

First, select the picture you want to crop. Then refer to the Picture toolbar. (If it isn't visible, pull down the View menu and click Toolbars, Picture.) Do the following:

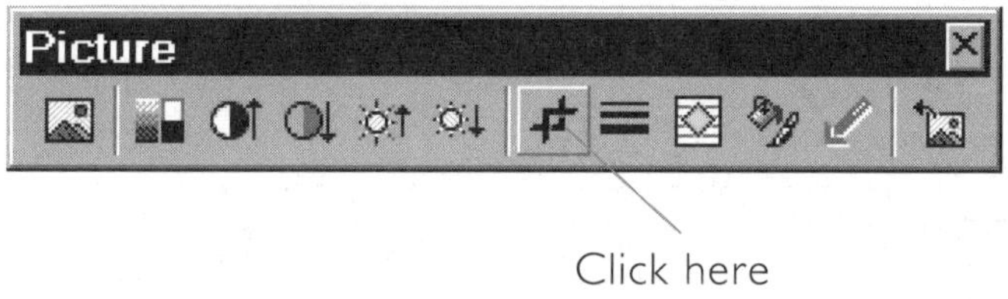

Now select the picture you want to crop. Move the mouse pointer over one of the available eight handles. Hold down the left mouse button and drag the handle inwards. Release the button to confirm the cropping operation.

Here, the image has been cropped using the centre right handle

Page setup – an overview

Word gives you great control over page layout. You can specify:

- the top, bottom, left and/or right page margins
- the distance between the top page edge and the top edge of the header
- the distance between the bottom page edge and bottom edge of the footer

The illustration below shows these page components:

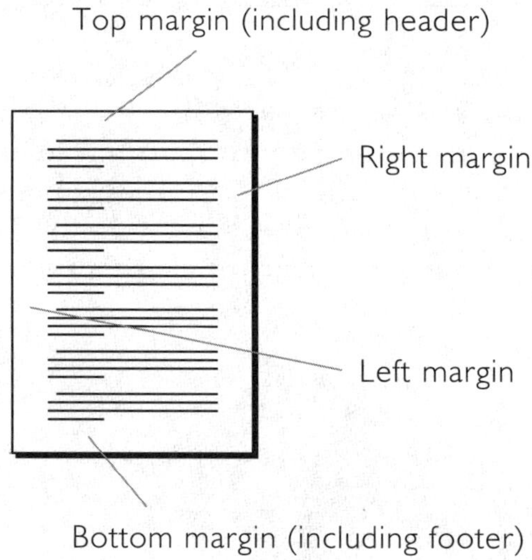

You can also specify:

- the page size (irrespective of margins and headers/ footers)
- the page orientation ('landscape' or 'portrait')

If none of the supplied page sizes is suitable, you can even customise your own.

HANDY TIP

See page 70 for a definition of landscape and portrait orientation.

Specifying margins

HANDY TIP

Margin settings are the framework on which indents and tabs are based.

All documents have margins, because printing on the whole of a sheet is both unsightly and, in the case of many printers (since the mechanism has to grip the page), impossible. Documents need a certain amount of 'white space' (the unprinted portion of the page) to balance the areas which contain text and graphics. Without this, they can't be visually effective. As a result, it's important to set margins correctly.

Customising margins

First, position the insertion point at the location within the active document from which you want the new margin(s) to apply. Alternatively, select the relevant portion of your document. Then pull down the File menu and click Page Setup. Carry out step 1 below. Then follow steps 2-5, as appropriate. Finally, carry out step 6.

1 Ensure the Margins tab is active

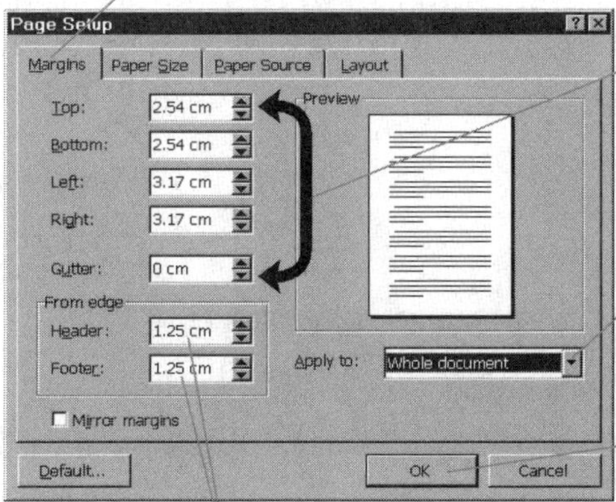

2 Type in the margin settings you need

4 Click here...

6 Click here

3 Type in header and/or footer margin settings

HANDY TIP

Re step 5 – if you selected text before launching this dialog, click Selected Text.

5 Then specify how much of the document you want the new margin(s) to affect

Specifying the page size

Word comes with some 17 preset page sizes – for instance, A4, A5 and Letter. These are suitable for most purposes. However, you can also set up your own page definition if you need to.

There are two aspects to every page size: a vertical measurement, and a horizontal measurement. These can be varied according to orientation. There are two possible orientations:

Whatever the page size, you can have both portrait and landscape pages in the same document.

To create your own page size, click Custom size in step 2. Then type in the desired measurements in the Width & Height fields. Finally, carry out step 4.

Setting the page size

First, position the insertion point at the location within the active document from which you want the new page size to apply. Then pull down the File menu and click Page Setup. Now do the following:

1 Ensure the Paper Size tab is active

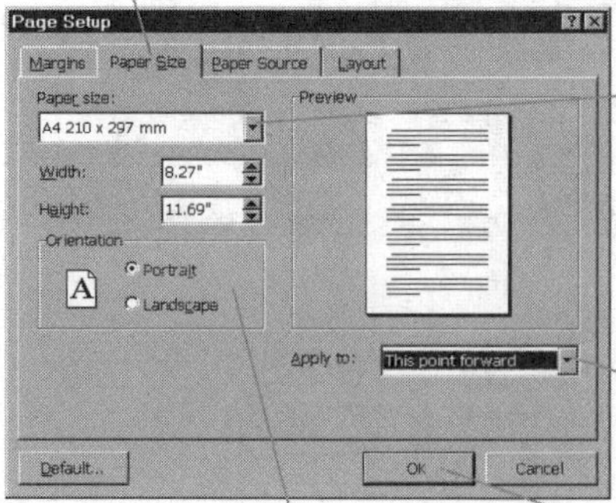

2 Click here; click the page size you need in the drop-down list

4 Click here; select 'This point forward' in the list

3 Click an orientation

5 Click here

Re step 4 – click Whole Document in the list to apply the new page size globally.

Using Print Preview

Word provides a special view mode called Print Preview. This displays the active document exactly as it will look when printed. Use Print Preview as a final check just before you print your document.

You can customise the way Print Preview displays your document in various ways. For example, you can:

- zoom in or out on the active page
- specify how many pages display
- hide almost everything on screen apart from the document

Launching Print Preview

Pull down the File menu and click Print Preview. This is the result:

HANDY TIP

To leave Print Preview mode and return to Normal, Online Layout or Page Layout view, simply press Esc.

Print Preview toolbar

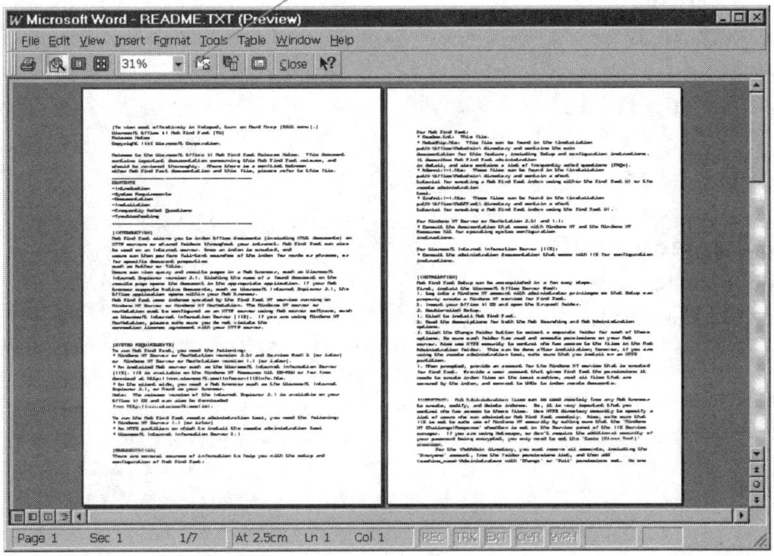

Zooming in or out in Print Preview

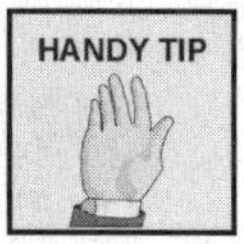

To view more than one page in Print Preview, click this button in the Print Preview toolbar:

Word launches a graphical list. Do the following:

Click and hold here

Now drag the mouse pointer to the right and/or down (the list expands as you do so). When you find the right page multiple (you can view as many as 18 pages at the same time), release the mouse button.

There are two ways in which you can change the display magnification in Print Preview mode.

Using the mouse

To magnify *part* of the active document, click the Magnifier button in the Print Preview toolbar.

Click here

The mouse pointer changes to a magnifying glass. Position this over the portion of the active document that you want to expand. Left-click once.

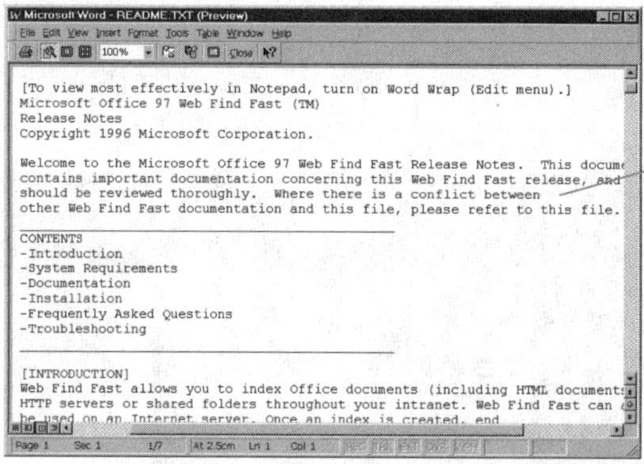

A magnified view of the upper central portion of the Print Preview screen

Using the Zoom Control button

To choose from pre-defined Zoom sizes, do the following:

1 Click here

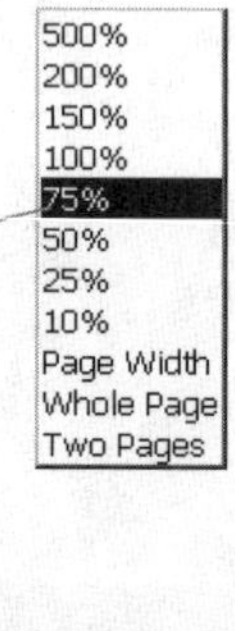

2 Click here

Clearing the screen in Print Preview

We saw earlier that it's possible to hide superfluous screen components in Normal, Online Layout and Page Layout views. You can also do this in Print Preview mode. Word calls this Full Screen view.

The advantage is that using Full Screen view in Print Preview mode makes more space available for display purposes. This is highly desirable unless you have a particularly large monitor. In Print Preview mode, Full Screen view hides all screen components except for the Print Preview toolbar, the dedicated Full Screen toolbar and (if applicable) the horizontal/vertical scroll bars.

Implementing Full Screen view

Refer to the Print Screen toolbar and do the following:

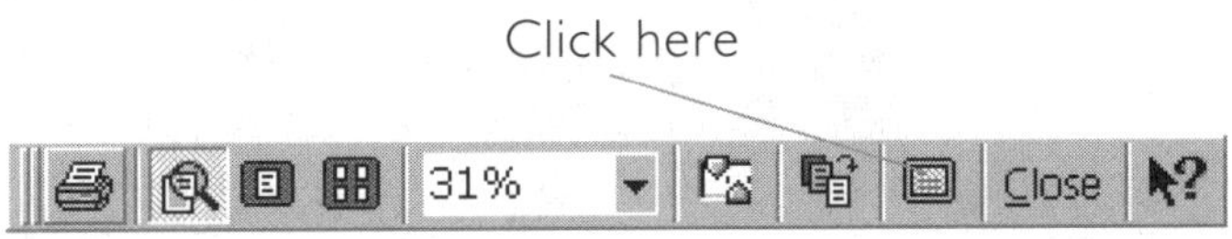

There is a keyboard shortcut you can use to leave Full Screen view: simply press Esc.

Alternatively, click the Full Screen toolbar:

To leave Full Screen view, repeat this procedure.

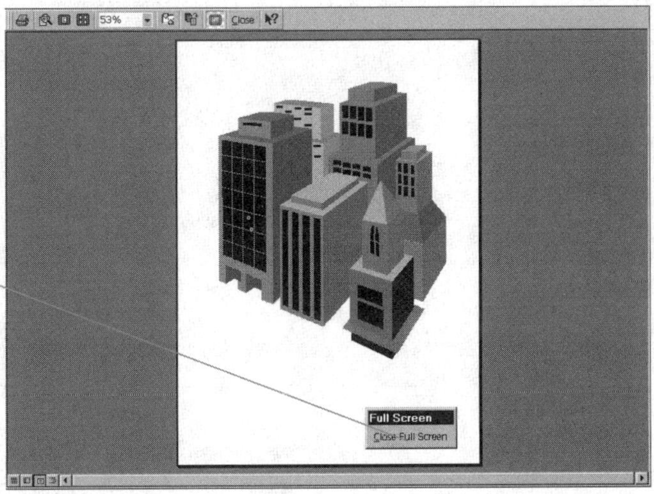

Printer setup

HANDY TIP **The question of which printer you select affects how the document displays in Print Preview mode.**

Most Word documents need to be printed eventually. Before you can begin printing, however, you need to ensure that:

- the correct printer is selected (if you have more than one installed)
- the correct printer settings are in force

Word calls these collectively the 'printer setup'.

Irrespective of the printer selected, the settings vary in accordance with the job in hand. For example, most printer drivers (the software which 'drives' the printer) allow you to specify whether or not you want pictures printed. Additionally, they often allow you to specify the resolution or print quality of the output...

Selecting the printer and/or settings

At any time before you're ready to print a document, pull down the File menu and click Print. Now do the following:

HANDY TIP **This procedure can also be followed from within Print Preview mode.**

1 Click here; select the printer you want from the list

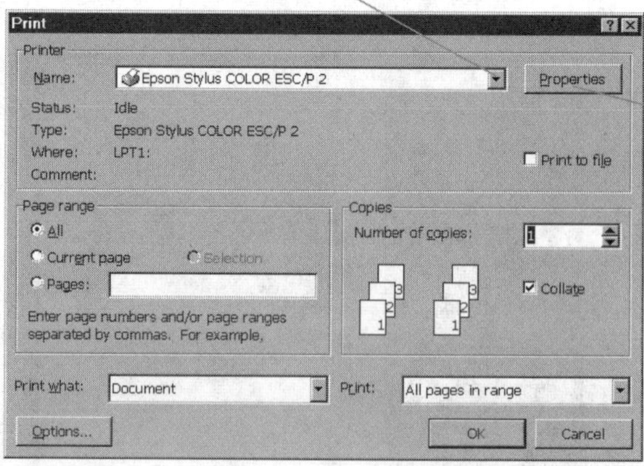

2 Click here to adjust printer settings (for how to do this, see your printer's manual)

Now complete the remainder of the Print dialog, prior to printing your document (see pages 77-78).

Printing – an overview

Once the active document is how you want it (and you've customised the printer setup appropriately), you'll probably need to print it out. Word makes this process easy and straightforward. It lets you set a variety of options before you do so.

Alternatively, you can simply opt to print your document with the default options in force (Word provides a 'fast track' approach to this).

Available print options include:

- the number of copies you want printed
- whether you want the copies 'collated'. This is the process whereby Word prints one full copy at a time. For instance, if you're printing three copies of a 40-page document, Word prints pages 1-40 of the first document, followed by pages 1-40 of the second and pages 1-40 of the third.
- which pages (or page ranges) you want printed
- whether you want to limit the print run to odd or even pages
- whether you want the print run restricted to text you selected before initiating printing
- whether you want the pages printed in reverse order (e.g. from the last page to the first)
- the quality of the eventual output (with many printers, Word allows you to print with minimal formatting for proofing purposes)
- whether you want to go on working in Word while the document prints (the default). Word calls this 'background printing'.

You can 'mix and match' these, as appropriate.

Printing – the fast track approach

Since documents and printing needs vary dramatically, it's often necessary to customise print options before you begin printing.

For example, if you've created a document which contains numerous pictures, you may well want to print out a draft copy for proofing purposes prior to printing the final version (although Print Preview mode provides a very effective indication of how a document will look when printed, there are still errors which are only detectable when you're working with hard copy). In this situation, you may wish to exclude pictures or print with minimal formatting. (For how to set your own print options, see the 'Customised printing (1)' and 'Customised printing (2)' topics later.)

On the other hand, simple documents can often benefit from a simple approach. In this case, you may well be content to print using the default options. Word recognises this and provides a method which bypasses the standard Print dialog, and is therefore much quicker and easier to use.

Printing with the current print options

First, ensure your printer is ready and on-line. Make sure the Standard toolbar is visible. (If it isn't, pull down the View menu and click Toolbars, Standard.) Now do the following:

Word starts printing the active document immediately.

Customised printing (1)

HANDY TIP

If you need to print in reverse order or with minimal formatting (or if you want to turn off background printing), follow the procedures under 'Customised printing (2)' before you carry out step 6 here.

HANDY TIP

Re step 3 – separate non-adjacent pages with commas but no spaces – e.g. to print pages 5, 12, 16 and 19 type:

5,12,16,19

Enter contiguous pages with dashes – e.g. to print pages 12 to 23 inclusive, type:

12-23

You can use a mix-and-match approach – e.g. to print pages 5, 6, 13-18 inclusive and 23, type:

5,6,13-18,23

If you need to set revised print options before printing, do the following.

Pull down the File menu and click Print. Now carry out steps 1-5, as appropriate. Finally, carry out step 6.

1 Click here to deselect collation

2 Type in the number of copies

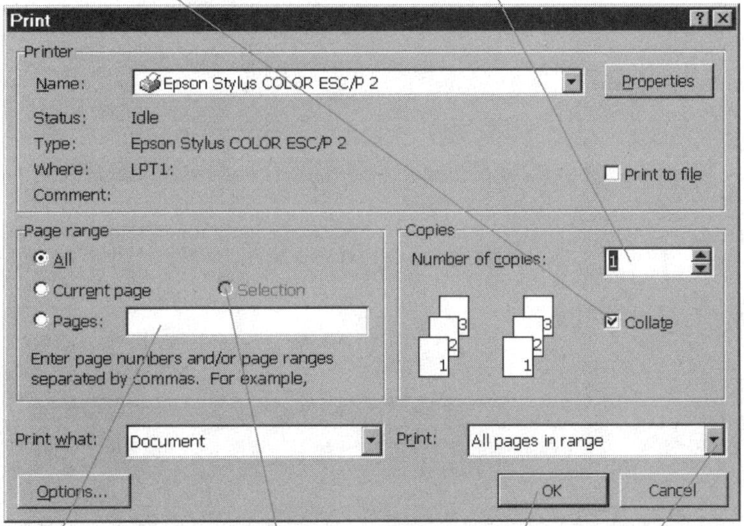

3 Type in the relevant page range (see tip opposite)

4 Click here if you selected text before launching this dialog and this is all you want to print

6 Click here

5 To print only odd or even pages, click here; select Odd Pages or Even Pages

Word starts printing the active document.

Customised printing (2)

Other print options are accessible from within a special dialog. This is launched from within the Print dialog.

First, pull down the File menu and click Print. Then do the following:

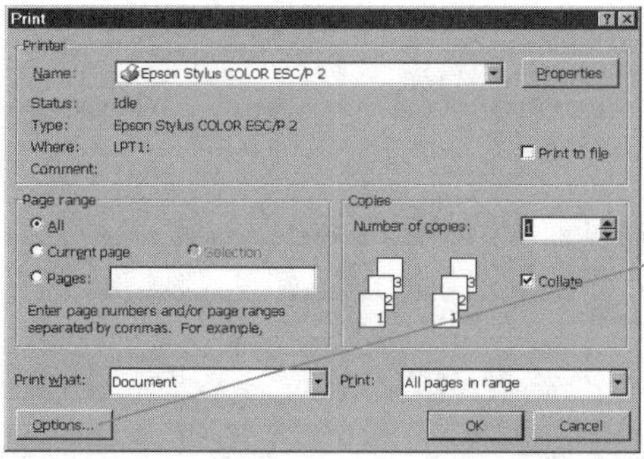

Click here

Now carry out steps 1-3 below (as appropriate), then step 4.

1 Click here to print with minimal formatting

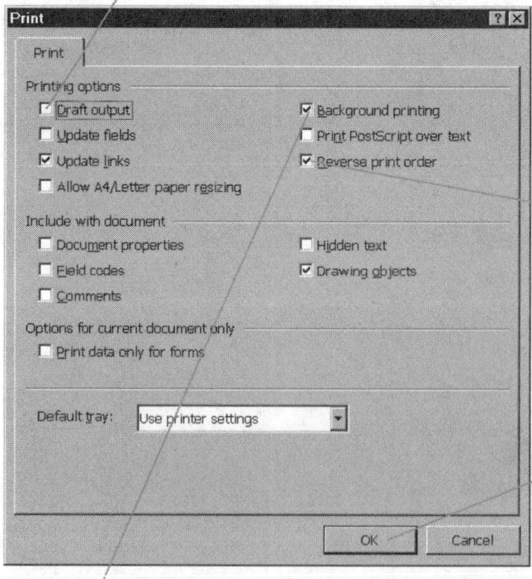

3 Ensure this is selected to print pages in reverse order

4 Click here

2 Click here to turn off background printing

Step 4 returns you to the Print dialog. Now follow step 6 under 'Customised printing (1)' to initiate printing.

Chapter Three

Excel

This chapter gives you the fundamentals of using Excel. You'll learn how to work with data and formulas, and how to move around worksheets. You'll also learn how to insert pictures, and make your data more visually effective by viewing it as a chart. Finally, you'll customise worksheet layout, preview your work and then print it out.

Covers

The Excel screen

Below is a detailed illustration of the Excel screen.

REMEMBER

This is a floating toolbar, specific to the invoice worksheet:

REMEMBER

This is the worksheet tab area. The screen components here are used to move through Excel documents.

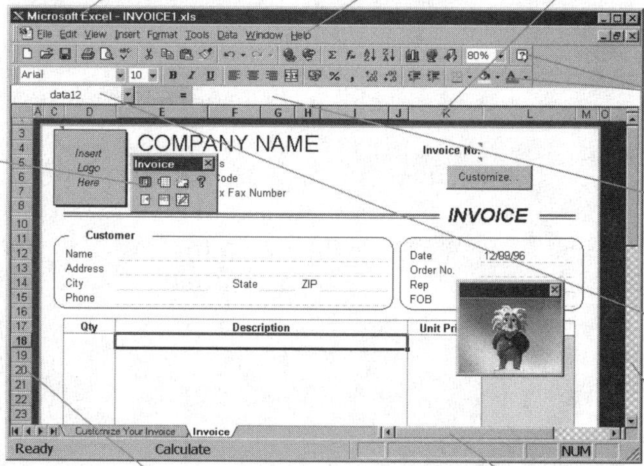

Some of these screen components can be hidden at will.

Specifying which screen components display

Pull down the Tools menu and click Options. Then:

1. Ensure the View tab is active

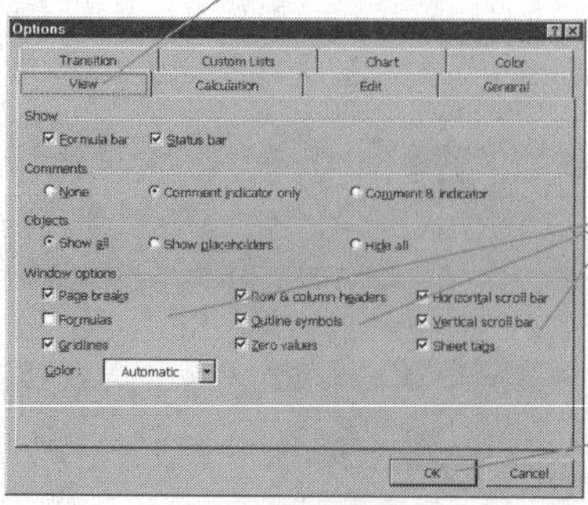

2. Click any feature in the Window options section to select or deselect it
3. Click here

HANDY TIP

Repeat step 2 for as many Window options as you want to select or deselect.

Entering data (1)

When you start Excel, you're presented with a new blank spreadsheet:

HANDY TIP **When you run Excel, you're actually opening a new workbook (see the main text below). Excel calls these 'Book 1', 'Book 2' etc.**

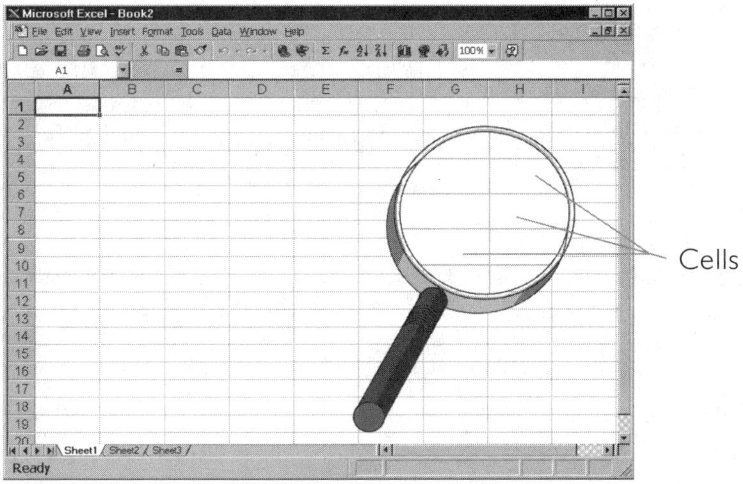

This means that you can start entering data immediately.

In Excel, you can enter the following basic data types:

- values (i.e. numbers)
- text (e.g. headings and explanatory material)
- functions (e.g. Sine or Cosine)
- formulas (combinations of values, text and functions)

REMEMBER **Columns are vertical, rows horizontal. Each worksheet can have as many as 256 columns and 65,536 rows, making a grand total of 16,777,216 cells.**

You enter data into 'cells'. Cells are formed where rows and columns intersect (see the illustration above).

Collections of rows/columns and cells are known in Excel as worksheets. Worksheets are organised into workbooks (by default, each workbook has 3 worksheets). Workbooks are the files that are stored on disk when you save your work in Excel.

Entering data (2)

HANDY TIP **When you enter values which are too big (physically) to fit in the holding cell, Excel inserts:**

#####

To resolve this, widen the column (see the 'Amending row/column sizes' topic later). Or pull down the Format menu and click Column, Autofit Selection to have Excel automatically increase the column size to match the contents.

Although you can enter data *directly* into a cell (by simply clicking in the cell and typing it in), there's another method you can use which is often easier. Excel provides a special screen component known as the Formula bar.

The illustration below shows the end of a blank worksheet. Some sample text has been inserted into cell IV65536 (note that the Name box tells you which cell is currently active).

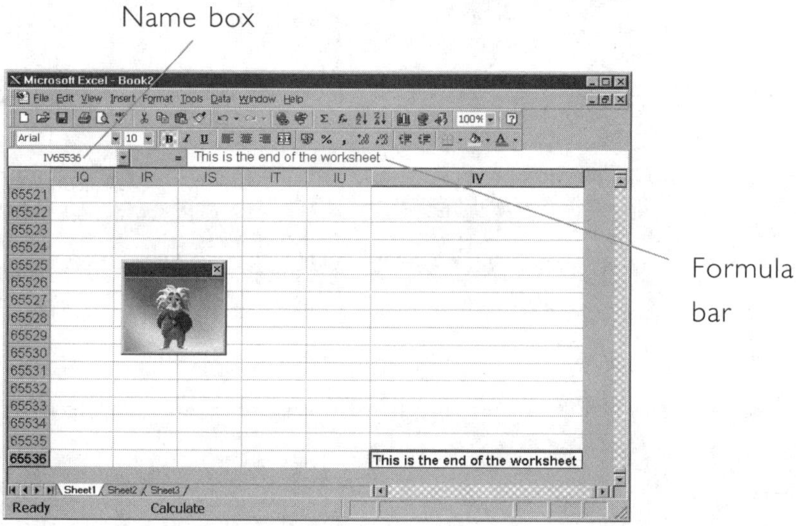

Entering data via the Formula bar

Click the cell you want to insert data into. Then click the Formula bar. Type in the data. Then follow step 1 below. If you decide not to proceed with the operation, follow step 2 instead:

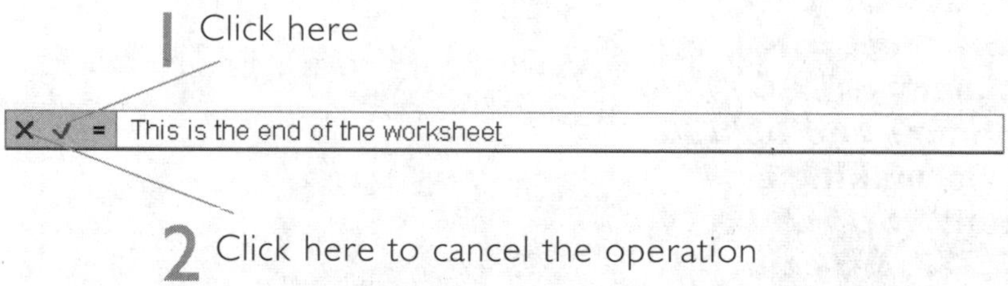

HANDY TIP **You can use a keyboard route to confirm operations in the Formula bar: simply press Return.**

Modifying existing data

HANDY TIP

Excel now supports multiple undos and redos. To undo one or more editing actions, do the following:

in the Standard toolbar. Make your selection in the list and press Enter.

To redo one or more actions, do the following:

in the Standard toolbar. Make your selection in the list and press Enter.

You can amend the contents of a cell in two ways:

- via the Formula bar
- from within the cell

When you use either of these methods, Excel enters a special state known as Edit Mode.

Amending existing data using the Formula bar

Click the cell whose contents you want to change. Then click in the Formula bar. Make the appropriate revisions and/or additions. Then press Return. Excel updates the relevant cell.

Amending existing data internally

Click the cell whose contents you want to change. Press F2. Make the appropriate revisions and/or additions *within the cell*. Then press Return.

The illustration below shows a section of a workbook created with the template INVOICE.XLT supplied with Excel.

A magnified view of cell K18, in Edit Mode

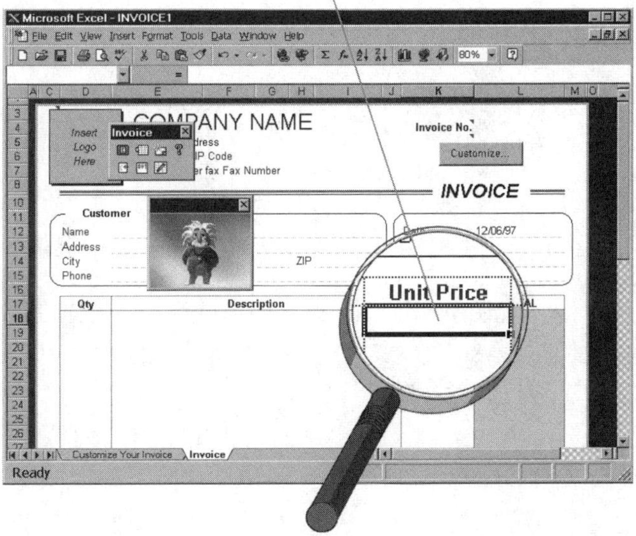

Working with cell ranges

When you're working with more than one cell, it's often convenient and useful to organise them in 'ranges'.

A range is a rectangular arrangement of cells. In the illustration below, cells A3, A4, A5, A6, B3, B4, B5 and B6 have been selected.

A selected cell range

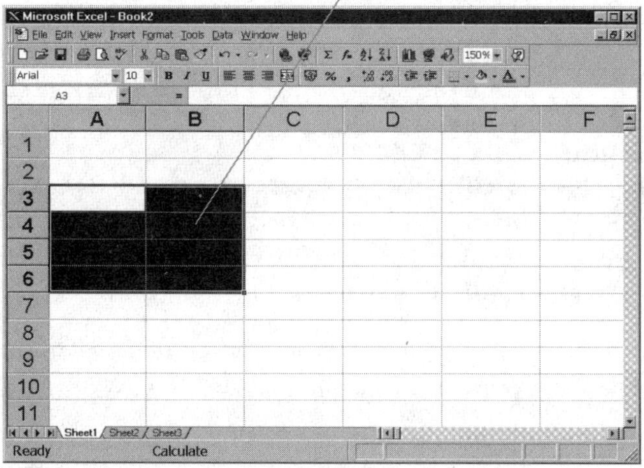

HANDY TIP

You can also use additional reference shortcuts – use the following as guides:

All cells in row 15 *15:15*

All cells in rows 8 to 20 *8:20*

All cells in column A *A:A*

All cells in columns P to S *P:S*

The above description of the relevant cells is very cumbersome. It's much more useful to use a form of shorthand. Excel (using the start and end cells as reference points) refers to these cells as:

A3:B6

You can extend this even more. Cell addresses can also incorporate a component which refers to the worksheet that contains the range. For example, to denote that the range A3:B6 is in worksheet 8, you'd use:

Sheet8!A3:B6

Moving around in worksheets (1)

Excel worksheets are huge. Moving to cells which happen to be visible is easy: you simply click in the relevant cell. However, Excel provides several techniques you can use to jump to less accessible areas.

HANDY TIP When you carry out steps 1 and 2 on the right, Excel displays a bubble showing where you're up to:

Using the scroll bars

Use any of the following methods:

1. to scroll quickly to another section of the active worksheet, drag the scroll box along the scroll bar until you reach it
2. to move one window to the right or left, click to the left or right of the scroll box in the horizontal scroll bar
3. to move one window up or down, click above or below the scroll box in the vertical scroll bar
4. to move up or down by one row, click the arrows in the vertical scroll bar
5. to move left or right by one column, click the arrows in the horizontal scroll bar

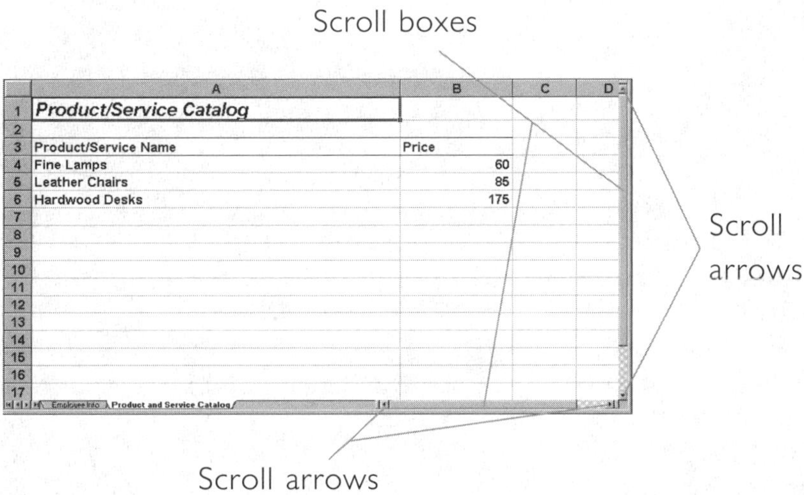

Moving around in worksheets (2)

HANDY TIP

Excel facilitates worksheet navigation. As you move the insertion point from cell to cell, the relevant row and column headers are emboldened:

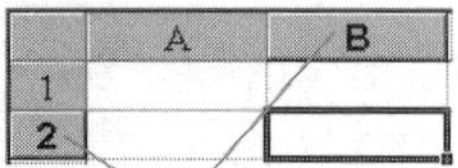

Emboldened headers

Using the keyboard

You can use the following techniques:

1. use the cursor keys to move one cell left, right, up or down.
2. hold down Ctrl as you use 1. above; this jumps to the edge of the current section (e.g. if cell B11 is active and you hold down Ctrl as you press ➔, Excel jumps to IV11, the last cell in row 11).
3. press Home to jump to the first cell in the active row, or Ctrl+Home to move to A1.
4. press Page Up or Page Down to move up or down by one screen.
5. press Alt+Page Down to move one screen to the right, or Alt+Page Up to move one screen to the left.

HANDY TIP

You can use a keyboard shortcut to launch the Go To dialog: simply press F5, or Ctrl+G.

Using the Go To dialog

Excel provides a special dialog which you can use to specify precise cell destinations.

Pull down the Edit menu and click Go To. Now do the following:

REMEMBER

Re step 1 – a cell's 'reference' (or 'address') identifies it in relation to its position in a worksheet, e.g. B11 or H23. You can also type in cell ranges here.

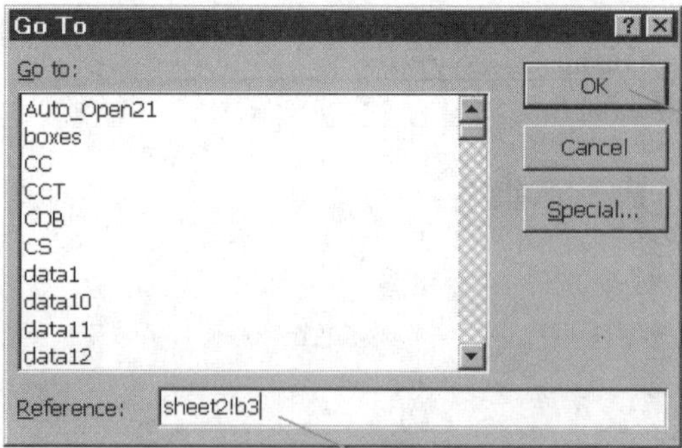

2 Click here

1 Type in the cell reference you want to move to

Switching between worksheets

Because workbooks have more than one worksheet, Excel provides two easy and convenient methods for moving between them.

Using the Tab area

You can use the Tab area (at the base of the Excel screen) to:

- jump to the first or last sheet
- jump to the next or previous sheet
- jump to a specific sheet

See the illustration below:

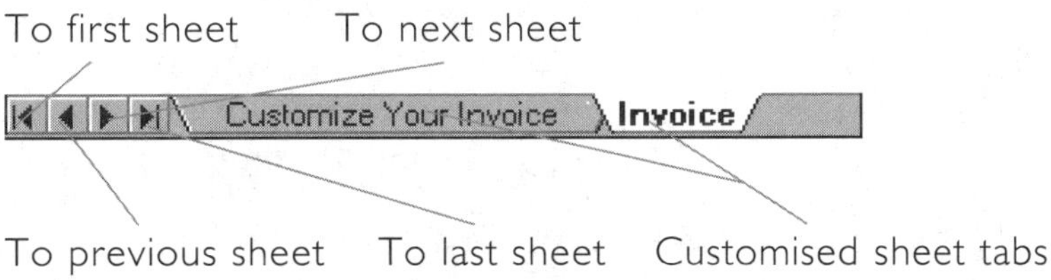

To move to a specific sheet, simply click the relevant tab.

An example: in the illustration above, to jump to the 'Customize Your Invoice' worksheet, simply click the appropriate tab.

When you click a worksheet tab, Excel emboldens the name and makes the tab background white.

Using the keyboard

You can use a keyboard shortcut here.

Ctrl+Page Up	moves to the previous tab
Ctrl+Page Down	moves to the next tab

Other operations on worksheets (1)

We said earlier that, by default, each workbook has three worksheets. However, you can easily:

- add new worksheets
- delete existing worksheets
- move existing worksheets

Inserting a single worksheet

In the worksheet tab area at the base of the screen, click the tab which represents the sheet in front of which you want the new worksheet inserted. Pull down the Insert menu and click Worksheet.

You can use a keyboard shortcut to insert a worksheet: simply press Shift+F11.

Inserting more than one worksheet

To add multiple worksheets, hold down one Shift key as you click the required number of sheet tabs (in other words, to add six new worksheets, shift-click six tabs). Then pull down the Insert menu and click Worksheet.

Deleting worksheets

In the worksheet tab area, click a single worksheet tab (or shift-click multiple tabs to delete more than one worksheet at a time). Pull down the Edit menu and click Delete Sheet. Excel launches a special message. Do the following:

When you delete a worksheet, you automatically erase the worksheet contents, too.

Click here to proceed with the deletion

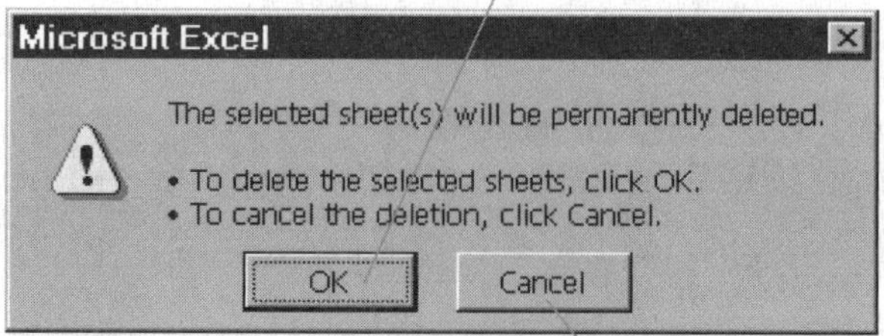

Or here to cancel it and return to your workbook

Other operations on worksheets (2)

You can perform two kinds of move operation on worksheets. You can:

- rearrange the worksheet order within a given workbook
- transfer a worksheet to another workbook

Rearranging worksheets

To select a single worksheet, click the relevant sheet tab in the worksheet tab area; or select more than one worksheet by holding down one Shift key as you click multiple tabs. With the mouse pointer still over the selected tab(s), hold down the left mouse button and drag them to their new location. Release the mouse button to confirm the operation.

Moving worksheets to another workbook

To select a single worksheet, click the relevant sheet tab in the worksheet tab area; or select more than one worksheet by holding down one Shift key as you click multiple tabs. Pull down the Edit menu and click Move or Copy Sheet. Now do the following:

1 Click here; select the new host workbook from the drop-down list

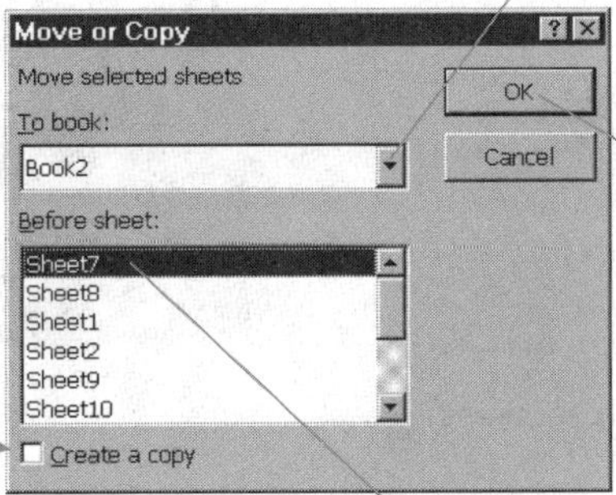

3 Click here

2 Click the worksheet in front of which you want the transferred sheet(s) to appear

HANDY TIP

Click here to perform a copy operation rather than a move.

Selection techniques

With the exception of the first cell, a selected range is filled with black.

You can also use another keyboard route.

Place the cell pointer in the first cell. Press F8. Use the cursor keys to define the selection. Finally, press F8 again.

You can use a keyboard shortcut to select every cell automatically: simply press Ctrl+A.

To select a row or column, do the following:

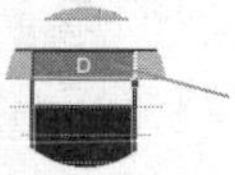

Click a column header

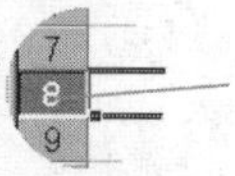

Click a row header

Before you can carry out any editing operations on cells in Excel, you have to select them first. Selecting a single cell is very easy: you merely click in it. However, Excel provides a variety of selection techniques which you can use to select more than one cell.

Selecting adjacent cell ranges

The easiest way to do this is to use the mouse. Click in the first cell in the range; hold down the left mouse button and drag over the remaining cells. Release the mouse button.

You can use the keyboard, too. Position the cell pointer over the first cell in the range. Hold down one Shift key as you use the relevant cursor key to extend the selection. Release the keys when the correct selection has been defined.

Selecting separate cell ranges

Excel lets you select more than one range at a time. Look at the illustration below:

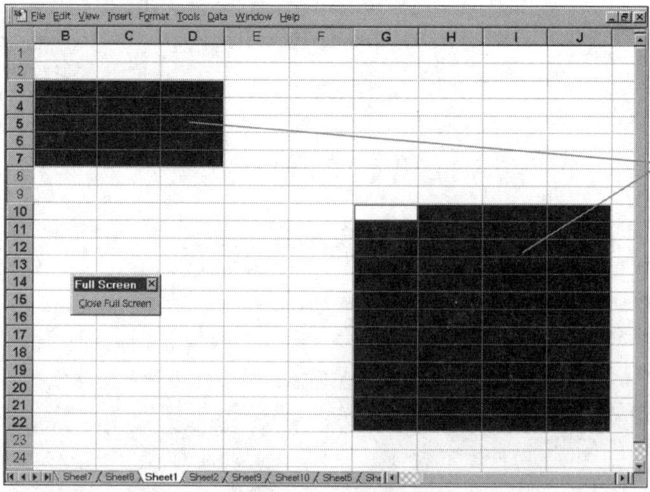

Two selected ranges

To select joint ranges, select the first in the normal way (you can't use the 'F8' method here). Then hold down Ctrl as you select subsequent ranges.

Formulas – an overview

Formulas are cell entries which define how other values relate to each other.

As a very simple example, consider the following:

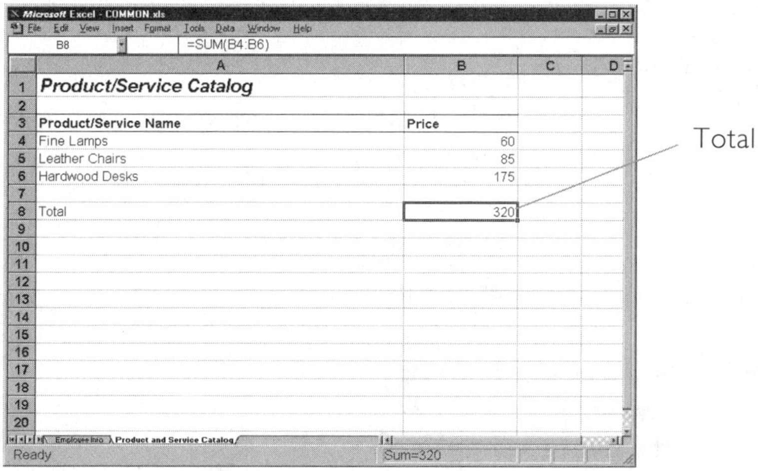

Here, a cell has been defined which returns the total of cells B4:B6. Obviously, in this instance you could insert the total easily enough yourself because the individual values are so small, and because we're only dealing with a small number of cells. But what happens if the cell values are larger and/or more numerous, or – more to the point – if they're liable to change frequently?

The solution is to insert a formula which carries out the necessary calculation automatically.

If you look at the Formula bar in the illustration, you'll see the formula which does this:

=SUM(B4:B6)

Many Excel formulas are much more complex than this, but the principles remain the same.

Inserting a formula

REMEMBER **Arguments (e.g. cell references) relating to functions are always contained in brackets.**

All formulas in Excel begin with an equals sign. This is usually followed by a permutation of the following:

- an operand (cell reference, e.g. B4)
- a function (e.g. the summation function, SUM)
- an arithmetical operator (+, –, / and *)
- comparison operators (<, >, <=, >= and =)

Excel supports a very wide range of functions organised into numerous categories. For more information on how to insert functions, see the 'Inserting a function' topic.

The mathematical operators are (in the order in which they appear in the bulleted list): *plus, minus, divide* and *multiply.*

The comparison operators are (in the order in which they appear in the list): *less than, greater than, less than or equal to, greater than or equal to* and *equals.*

There are two ways to enter formulas:

Entering a formula directly into the cell

Click the cell in which you want to insert a formula. Then type =, followed by your formula. When you've finished, press Return.

Entering a formula into the Formula bar

This is usually the most convenient method.

Click the cell in which you want to insert a formula. Then click in the Formula bar. Type =, followed by your formula. When you've finished, press Return or do the following:

Click here

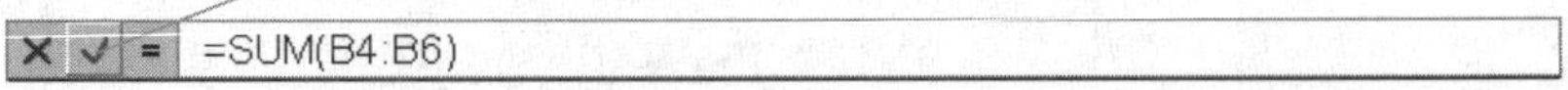

HANDY TIP **To enter a formula into every cell within a range, select the range, type the formula and then press Ctrl+Enter.**

Note, however, that Excel adjusts the formula intelligently. For instance, if range B9:D12 is selected and the formula =SUM(B2:B4) **inserted, the operands are incremented:**

Updated formulas

Inserting a function

HANDY TIP **Excel organises its functions under convenient headings – some examples are:**
Financial
Date & Time
Statistical
Text

Functions are pre-defined tools which accomplish specific tasks. These tasks are often calculations; occasionally, however, they're more generalised (e.g. some functions simply return dates and/or times). In effect, functions replace one or more formulas.

Excel provides a special dialog – the Formula Palette – to help ensure that you enter functions correctly. This is useful for the following reasons:

- Excel provides so many functions, it's convenient to apply them from a centralised source
- the Formula Palette ensures the functions are entered with the correct syntax

Functions can only be used in formulas.

HANDY TIP **You can also use another route to insert a function.**
Click in a cell. Pull down the Insert menu and click Function. In the Function category field in the Paste Function dialog, select a heading. Click a function in the Function name box. Click OK.
Excel now launches the Formula Palette – complete steps 2 and 3.

Inserting a function with the Formula Palette

At the relevant juncture during the process of inserting a formula, refer to the Formula bar and do the following:

Click here

Now carry out the following steps:

1 Click here; select a function from the list

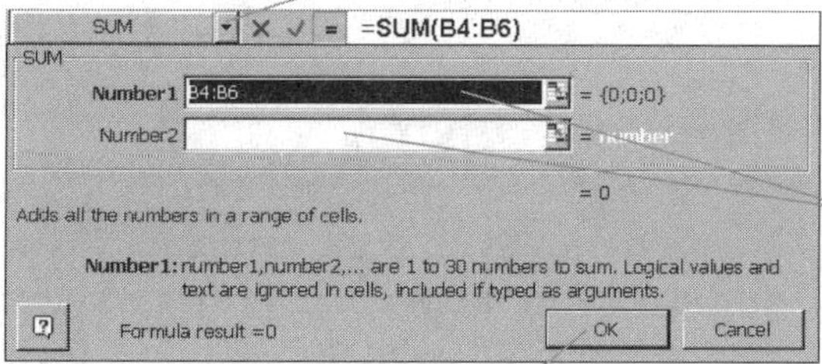

2 Enter the function arguments

3 Click here

Amending row/column sizes

Sooner or later, you'll find it necessary to change the width of rows or columns. This necessity arises when there is too much data in cells to display adequately. You can enlarge or shrink single or multiple rows/columns.

Changing row height

To change one row's height, click the row heading. If you want to change multiple rows, hold down Ctrl and click the appropriate extra headings. Then place the mouse pointer just under the row heading(s). Hold down the left mouse button and drag up or down to decrease or increase the row(s) respectively. Release the mouse button to confirm the operation.

Excel has a useful 'best fit' feature. Simply double-click just below the selected row headings, or to the right of selected column headings, to have the rows or columns adjust themselves automatically to their contents.

Drag here to amend rows 4, 5 and 6 jointly

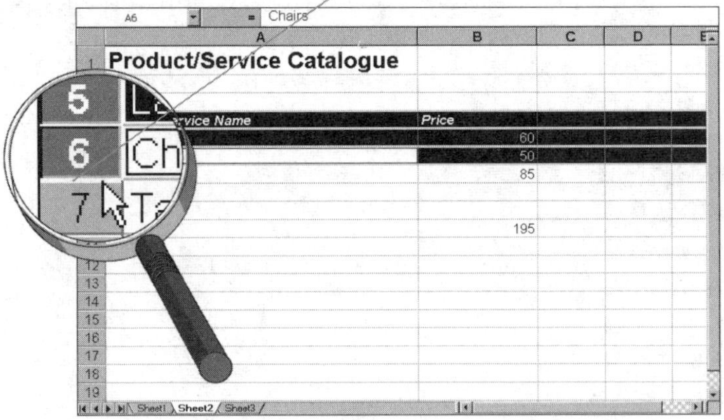

Changing column width

To change one column's width, click the column heading. If you want to change multiple columns, hold down Ctrl and click the appropriate extra headings. Then place the mouse pointer over the line located just to the right of the column heading(s). Hold down the left mouse button and drag the line right or left to widen or narrow the column(s) respectively.

Release the mouse button to confirm the operation.

Inserting cells, rows or columns

You can insert additional cells, rows or columns into worksheets.

REMEMBER If you select cells in more than one row or column, Excel inserts the equivalent number of new rows or columns.

Inserting a new row or column

First, select one or more cells within the row(s) or column(s) where you want to carry out the insert operation. Now pull down the Insert menu and click Rows or Columns, as appropriate. Excel inserts the new row(s) or column(s) immediately.

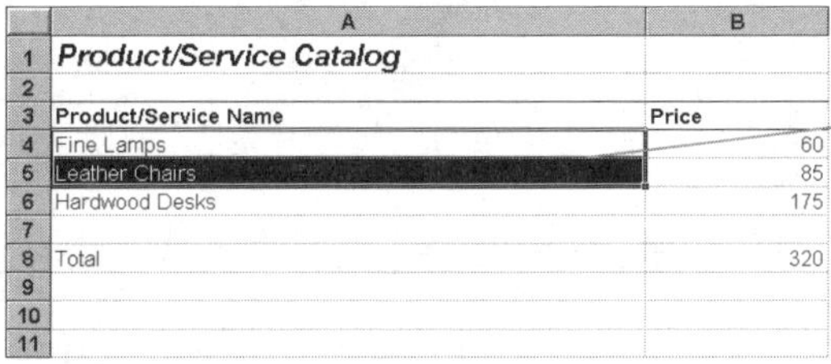

A worksheet extract. Here, one new column or two new rows are being added

Inserting a new cell range

Select the range where you want to insert the new cells. Pull down the Insert menu and click Cells. Now carry out step 1 or step 2 below. Finally, follow step 3.

1 Click here to have Excel make room for the new cells by moving the selected range *to the right*

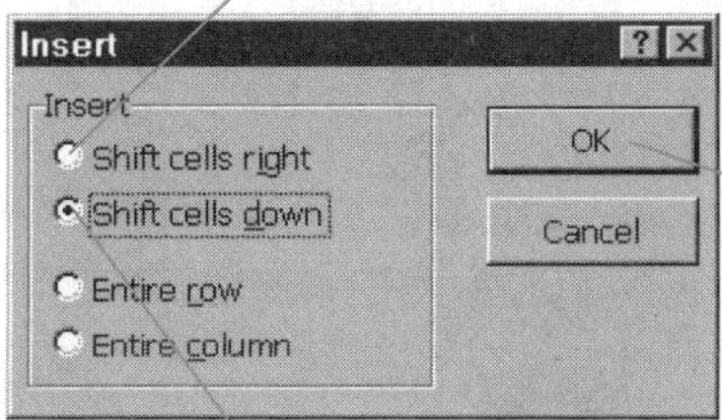

3 Click here

2 Click here to have Excel make room for the new cells by moving the selected range *down*

AutoFill

Types of series you can use AutoFill to complete include:

- 1st Period, 2nd Period etc.
- Mon, Tue, Wed etc.
- Quarter 1, Quarter 2 etc.
- Week1, Week2, Week 3 etc.

Excel lets you insert data series automatically. This is a very useful and timesaving feature. Look at the illustration below:

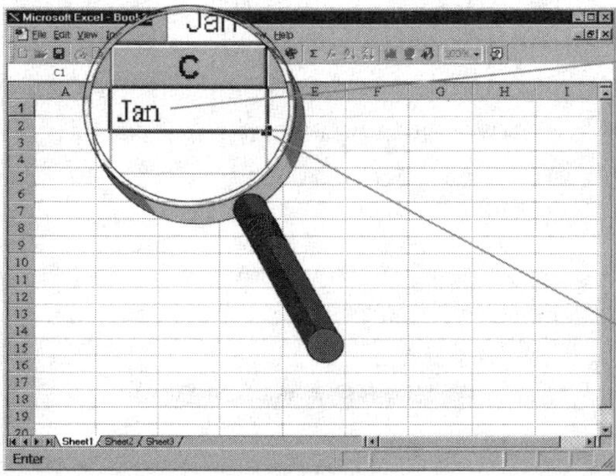

If you wanted to insert month names in successive cells in column A, you could do so manually. But there's a much easier way. You can use Excel's AutoFill feature.

Using AutoFill to create a series

Type in the first element(s) of the series in consecutive cells. Select the cells. Then position the mouse pointer over the Fill handle in the bottom right-hand corner of the last cell (the pointer changes to a crosshair). Hold down the left mouse button and drag the handle over the cells into which you want to extend the series (in the example here, over C2:C12). When you release the mouse button, Excel extrapolates the initial entry or entries into the appropriate series.

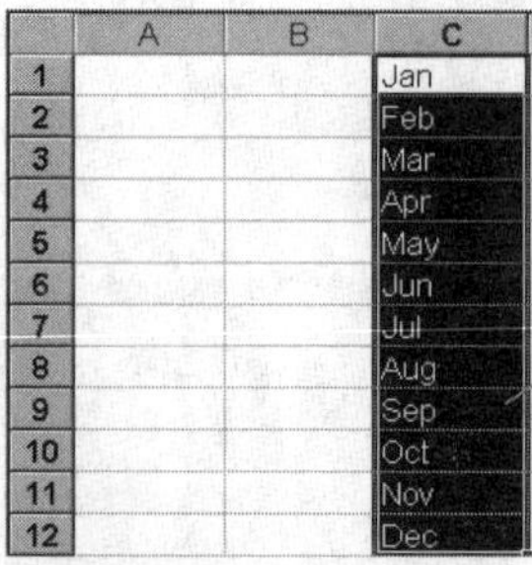

Changing number formats

Excel lets you apply formatting enhancements to cells and their contents. You can:

- specify a number format
- customise the font, type size and style of contents
- specify cell alignment
- border and/or shade cells

Specifying a number format

You can customise the way cell contents (e.g. numbers and dates/times) display in Excel. For example, you can specify at what point numbers are rounded up. Available formats are organised under several general categories. These include: Number, Accounting and Fraction.

Select the cells whose contents you want to customise. Pull down the Format menu and click Cells. Now do the following:

Re step 3 – the options you can choose from vary according to the category chosen. Complete them as necessary.

1 Ensure the Number tab is active

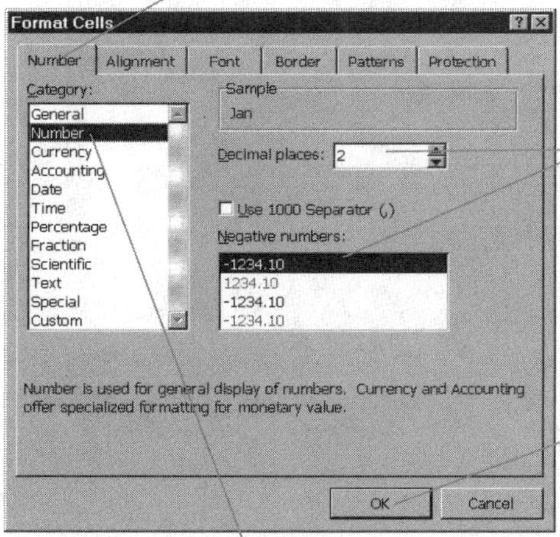

3 Complete the relevant options

4 Click here

2 Click a category

Changing fonts and styles

Excel lets you carry out the following actions on cell contents (numbers and/or text):

- apply a new font and/or type size
- apply a font style (for most fonts, you can choose from: Regular, Italic, Bold or Bold Italic)
- apply a colour
- apply a special effect (underlining, ~~strikethrough~~, superscript or subscript)

Amending the appearance of cell contents

Select the cell(s) whose contents you want to reformat. Pull down the Format menu and click Cells. Carry out step 1 below. Now follow any of steps 2-5, as appropriate, or either or both of the two tips. Finally, carry out step 6.

HANDY TIP

To underline the specified contents, click the arrow to the right of the Underline box; select an underlining type in the list.

HANDY TIP

To apply a special effect, click any of the options in the Effects section.

1 Ensure the Font tab is active

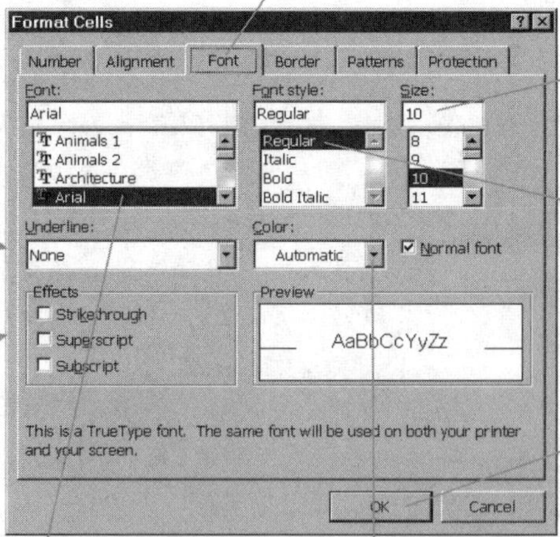

3 Enter a type size

5 Click the style you want to apply

6 Click here

2 Click the font you want to use

4 Click here; click the colour you want to apply in the list

Cell alignment (1)

By default, Excel aligns text to the left of cells, and numbers to the right. However, if you want you can change this.

You can specify alignment under two broad headings: Horizontal and Vertical.

REMEMBER

One further horizontal option – Center across selection – centres cell contents across more than one cell (if you selected a cell range before initiating it).

Horizontal alignment

The main options are:

General	the default (see above)
Left	contents are aligned to the left
Center	contents are centred
Right	contents are aligned to the right
Fill	contents are duplicated so that they fill the cell
Justify	a combination of Left and Right

Vertical alignment

Available options are:

Top	cell contents align with the top of the cell(s)
Center	contents are centred
Bottom	contents align with the cell bottom
Justify	contents are aligned along the top and bottom of the cell(s)

HANDY TIP

You can also rotate text within cells – see 'Cell alignment (2)' for more information.

Most of these settings parallel features found in Word (and – for that matter – in many other word-processors). The difference, however, lies in the fact that Excel has to align data within the bounds of cells rather than a page. When it aligns text, it often needs to employ its own version of text wrap. See the 'Cell alignment (2)' topic for more information on this.

Cell alignment (2)

Other alignment features you can set are rotation and text wrap.

Rotation controls the direction of text flow within cells; you achieve this by specifying a plus (anticlockwise) or minus (clockwise) angle.

When the Wrap Text option is selected, Excel – instead of overflowing any surplus text into adjacent cells to the right – forces it onto separate lines within the host cell.

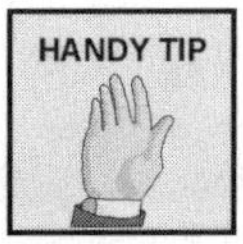

Re step 4 below – for an example of text rotated within the host cell (in this case, at an angle of 45°), see below:

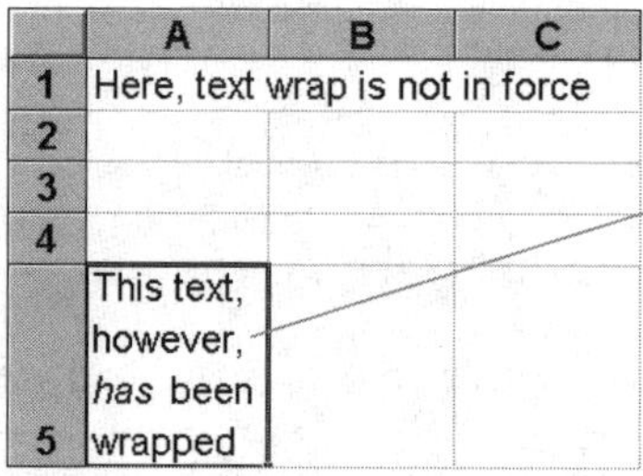

Text wrap in action

Customising cell alignment

Select the cell(s) whose contents you want to realign. Pull down the Format menu and click Cells. Carry out step 1 below. Now follow any or all of steps 2-4, as appropriate. Finally, carry out step 5.

Click here to wrap text within the holding cell(s):

1 Ensure the Alignment tab is active

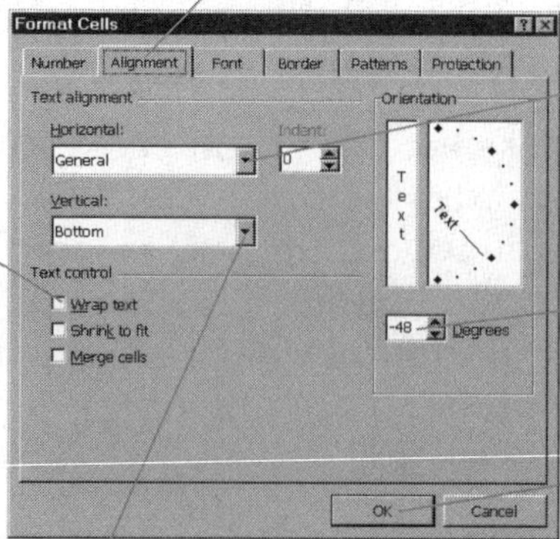

3 Click here; select a horizontal alignment from the list

4 Enter a rotation angle

5 Click here

2 Click here; select a vertical alignment from the list

Bordering cells

Excel lets you define a border around:

- the perimeter of a selected cell range
- specific sides within a cell range

You can customise the border by choosing from a selection of pre-defined border styles. You can also colour the border, if required.

Applying a cell border

First, select the cell range you want to border. Pull down the Format menu and click Cells. Now carry out steps 1 and 2 below. Step 3 is optional. Follow steps 4 and 5, as appropriate (if you're setting *multiple* border options, repeat steps 2-5 as required). Finally, carry out step 6:

HANDY TIP

Re step 5 – clicking any of the indicated buttons applies a border to just one side.

1 Ensure the Border tab is active

4 Click the relevant border style option

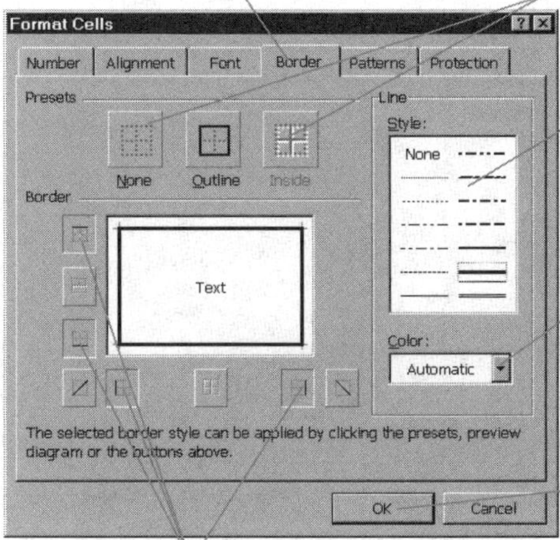

2 Click a preset line style

3 Click here; click the colour you want to apply in the list

6 Click here

5 Click the relevant border option(s) – see the tip.

Shading cells

Excel lets you apply the following to cells:

- a pattern
- a pattern colour
- a background colour

You can do any of these singly, or in combination. Interesting effects can be achieved by using pattern colours with coloured backgrounds.

Applying a pattern or background

First, select the cell range you want to shade. Pull down the Format menu and click Cells. Now carry out step 1. Perform step 2 to apply a *background* colour, and/or 3-4 to apply a *foreground* pattern or pattern/colour combination. Finally, follow step 5.

HANDY TIP **The Sample field previews how your background and pattern/colour will look.**

1 Ensure the Patterns tab is active

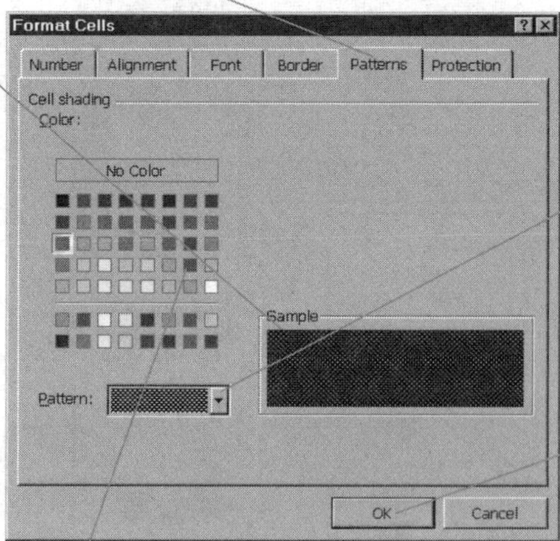

3 Click here to apply a pattern/ colour

5 Click here

2 Click a colour here to apply it as a background

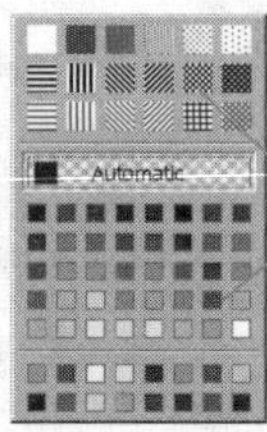

4 Click a pattern or colour

AutoFormat

Excel provides a shortcut to the formatting of worksheet data: AutoFormat.

AutoFormat consists of 16 pre-defined formatting schemes. These incorporate specific excerpts from the font, number, alignment, border and shading options discussed earlier. You can apply any of these schemes (and their associated formatting) to selected cell ranges with just a few mouse clicks. You can even specify which scheme elements you *don't* wish to use.

AutoFormat works with most arrangements of worksheet data.

Using AutoFormat

First, select the cell range you want to apply an automatic format to. Pull down the Format menu and click AutoFormat. Now carry out step 1 below. Steps 2 and 3 are optional. Finally, follow step 4.

HANDY TIP

The Sample field previews how your data will look with the specified AutoFormat.

4 Click here

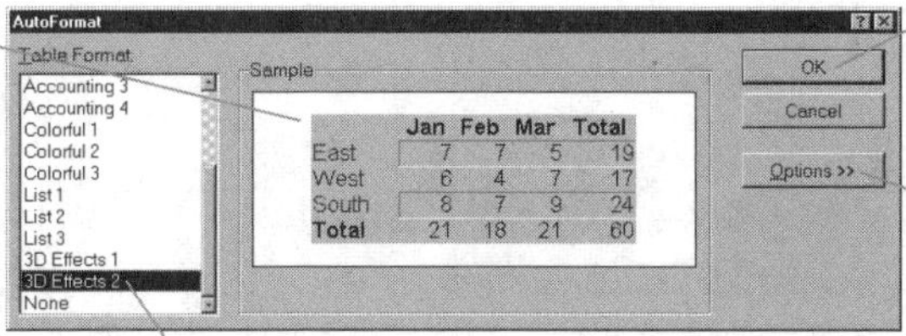

2 Click here to customise the format

1 Click the format you want to apply

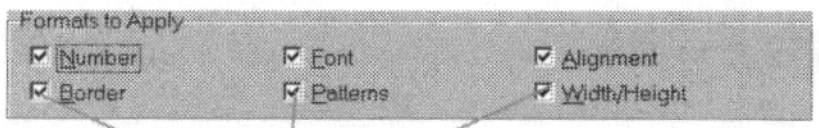

3 Click one or more options to omit them

Find operations

Excel lets you search for and jump to text or numbers (in short, any information) in your worksheets. This is a particularly useful feature when worksheets become large and complex.

You can organise your search by rows or by columns. You can also specify whether Excel looks in:

- cells that contain formulas
- cells that don't contain formulas

Additionally, you can insist that Excel only flag exact matches (i.e. if you searched for '11', Excel would not find '1111'), and you can also limit text searches to text which has the case you specified (e.g. searching for 'PRODUCT LIST' would not find 'Product List').

HANDY TIP **To search for data over more than one worksheet, select the relevant sheet tabs before following steps 1-6.**

Searching for data

Place the mouse pointer at the location in the active worksheet from which you want the search to begin. Pull down the Edit menu and click Find. Now carry out step 1 below, then any of steps 2-5. Finally, carry out step 6.

HANDY TIP **If you want to restrict the search to specific cells, select a cell range *before* you follow steps 1-6.**

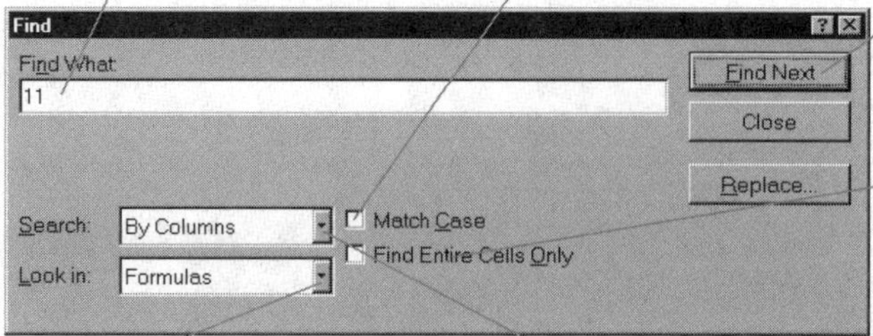

1 Type in the data you want to find

2 To limit the search, click here; select the relevant option from the list

3 To specify the search direction, click here; select the relevant option from the list

4 Click here for a case-specific search

5 For an exact match, click here

6 Click here

Find-and-replace operations

When you search for data, you can also – if you want – have Excel replace it with something else.

Find-and-replace operations can be organised by rows or by columns. However, unlike straight searches, you can't specify whether Excel looks in cells that contain formulas or those that don't. As with straight searches, you can, however, limit find-and-replace operations to exact matches and also (in the case of text) to precise case matches.

Normally, find-and-replace operations only affect the worksheet in which they're conducted. If you want to carry out an operation over multiple worksheets, see the tip.

HANDY TIP

To search for and replace data over more than one worksheet, select the relevant sheet tabs before following steps 1-8.

Running a find-and-replace operation

Place the mouse pointer at the location in the active worksheet from which you want the search to begin (or select a cell range if you want to restrict the find-and-replace operation to this). Pull down the Edit menu and click Replace. Now carry out step 1 below, then any of steps 2-5. Finally, carry out steps 6 and 7, OR 8.

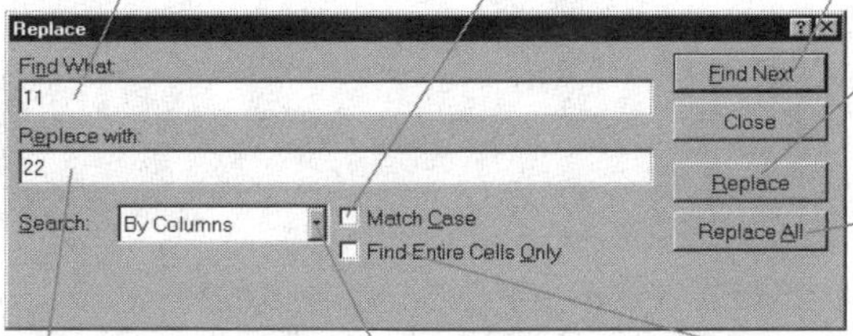

1 Type in the data you want to find

2 Type in the replacement data

3 To specify the search direction, click here; select the relevant option from the list

4 Click here for a case-specific search

5 For an exact match, click here

6 Click here to find the first occurrence

7 Click here to replace it

8 Click here to replace *all* occurrences

Charting – an overview

Excel has comprehensive charting capabilities, which enable you to convert selected data into its visual equivalent. To do this, Excel offers a wide number of chart formats and sub-formats.

HANDY TIP

You can add a picture to chart walls.

Select the wall(s) in the normal way. Then follow the procedures set out on page 109.

You can create a chart:

- as a picture within the parent worksheet
- as a separate chart sheet

Chart sheets have their own tabs in the tab area; these operate just like worksheet tabs.

Excel uses a special Wizard – ChartWizard – to make the process of creating charts as easy and convenient as possible.

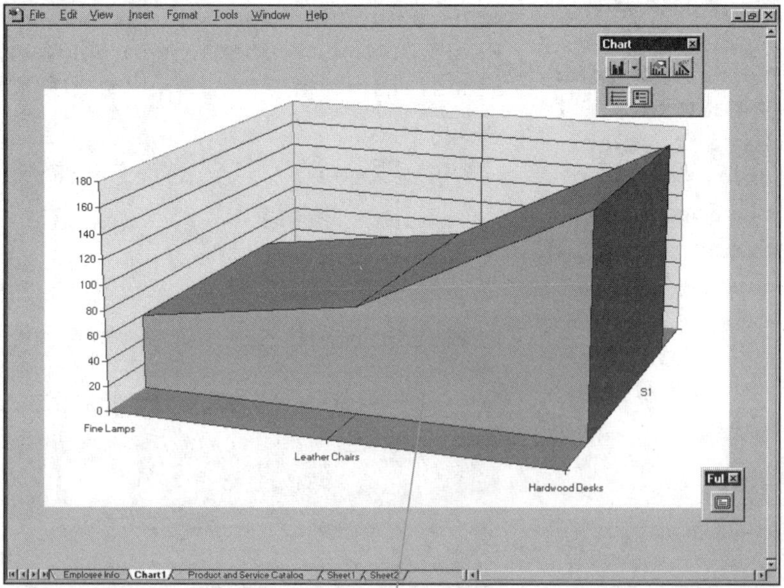

A 3-D Area chart

Creating a chart (1)

HANDY TIP

Click and hold here to have Excel preview the chart type/sub-type combination:

HANDY TIP

Click here: if you want the Office Assistant to supply help with chart creation.

First, select the cells you want converted into a chart. Pull down the Insert menu and click Chart. The first ChartWizard dialog appears. Do the following:

1 Click a chart type

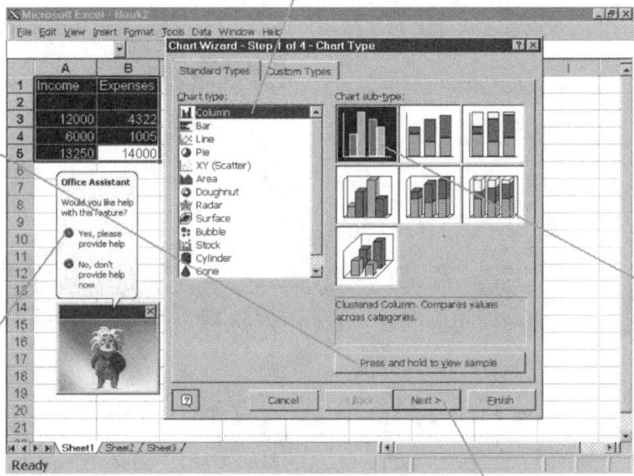

2 Click a chart sub-type

3 Click here

HANDY TIP

Re step 4 – click the Collapse Dialog button:

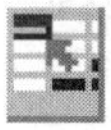

to hide the dialog temporarily while you select an alternative cell range.

When you've finished, do the following:

Click here

There are three more dialogs to complete. Carry out the following steps:

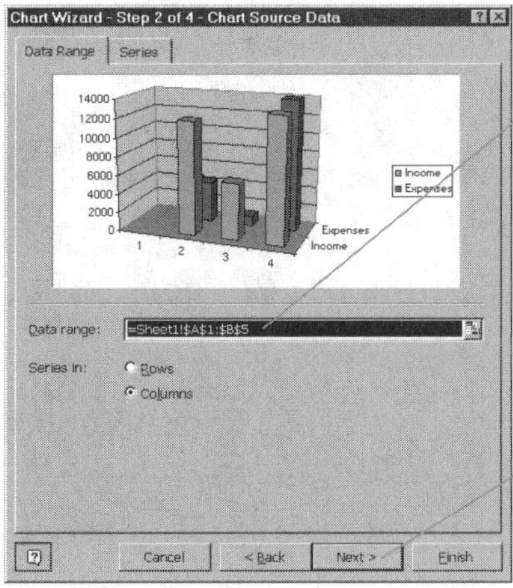

4 If you selected the wrong cells before launching the Chart Wizard, click here, then select the correct range in your worksheet

5 Click here

Creating a chart (2)

Excel launches the third ChartWizard dialog. Carry out the following steps:

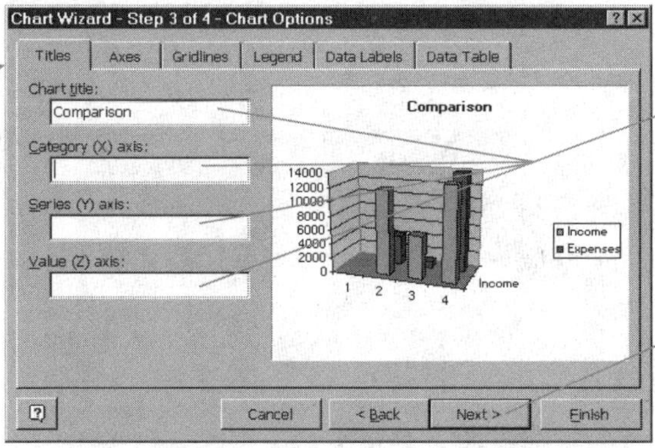

1 Optional – name the chart and/or axes

2 Click here

HANDY TIP

Click any of the additional tabs to set further chart options.

For example, activate the Gridlines tab to specify how and where gridlines display. Or click Legend to determine where legends (text labels) appear...

In the final dialog, you tell Excel whether you want the chart inserted into the current worksheet, or into a new chart sheet.

Carry out step 3 OR 4 below. Finally, perform step 5.

3 Click here to create a chart sheet

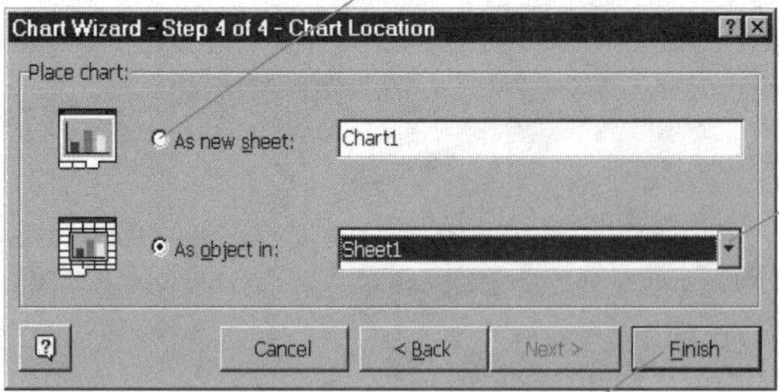

4 Click here; select an existing sheet in the list

5 Click here to generate the chart

Working with pictures

HANDY TIP

Once inserted into a worksheet, pictures can be resized and moved in the normal way.

HANDY TIP

You can also insert pictures onto chart walls – see page 106.

REMEMBER

Excel provides a preview of what the picture will look like when it's been imported. See the Preview box on the right of the dialog.

Most worksheets benefit from the inclusion of colour or greyscale pictures. These can be:

- output from other programs (e.g. drawings and illustrations)
- commercial clip art
- photographs

Excel will happily translate a wide variety of third-party graphics formats.

Inserting a picture

Position the insertion point at the location in the active worksheet where you want the picture to appear. Pull down the Insert menu and click Picture, From File. Now carry out the following steps:

2 Click here. In the drop-down list, click the drive/folder which hosts the picture

4 Click here

1 Make sure All Pictures is shown. If it isn't, click the arrow and select it from the drop-down list

3 Click a picture file

Page setup – an overview

HANDY TIP

Excel has a special view mode: – Page Break Preview – which you can also use to ensure your worksheet prints correctly.

Pull down the View menu and click Page Break Preview. Do the following (the white area denotes cells which will print, the grey those which won't):

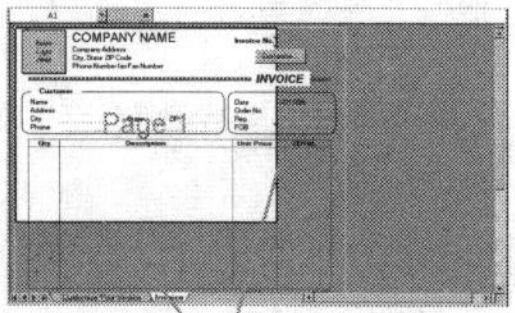

Drag page break margins to customise the printable area

REMEMBER

Charts in separate chart sheets have unique page setup options – see later.

Making sure your worksheets print with the correct page setup can be a complex issue, for the simple reason that most worksheets become very extensive with the passage of time (so large, in fact, that in the normal course of things they won't fit onto a single page).

Page setup features you can customise include:

- the paper size and orientation
- scaling
- the starting page number
- the print quality
- margins
- header/footer information
- page order
- which worksheet components print

Margin settings you can amend are:

- top
- bottom
- left
- right

Additionally, you can set the distance between the top page edge and the top of the header, and the distance between the bottom page edge and the bottom edge of the footer.

When you save your active workbook, all Page Setup settings are saved with it.

Setting page options

Excel comes with some 17 pre-defined paper sizes which you can apply to your worksheets, in either portrait (top-to-bottom) or landscape (sideways-on) orientation. This is one approach to effective printing. Another is scaling: you can print out your worksheets as they are, or you can have Excel shrink them so that they fit a given paper size (you can even automate this process). Additionally, you can set the print resolution and starting page number.

Using the Page tab in the Page Setup dialog

Pull down the File menu and click Page Setup. Now carry out step 1 below, followed by steps 2-6 as appropriate. Finally, carry out step 7:

HANDY TIP **Re step 5 – by default, Excel numbers pages from '1'. Leave the First Page Number field setting as Auto if you want this.**

HANDY TIP **To make your worksheet print in a specific number of pages, complete the Fit to field.**

1 Ensure the Page tab is active

2 Click the orientation you need

3 Click here; click the page size you need in the drop-down list

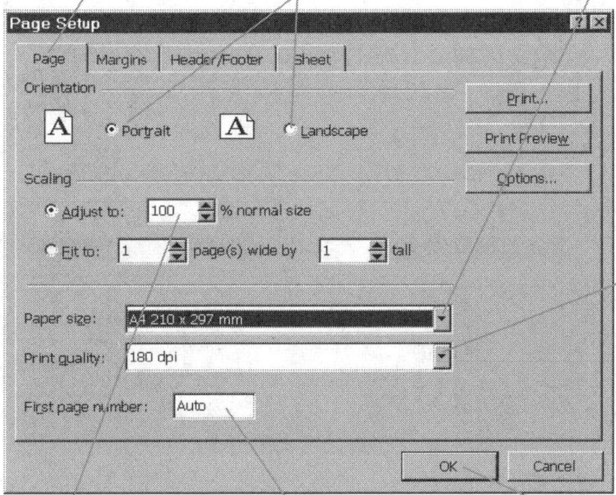

6 Click here; click the print quality you need in the drop-down list

4 Enter a scaling % here

5 Enter a page number to print from

7 Click here

Setting margin options

Excel lets you set a variety of margin settings. The illustration below shows the main ones:

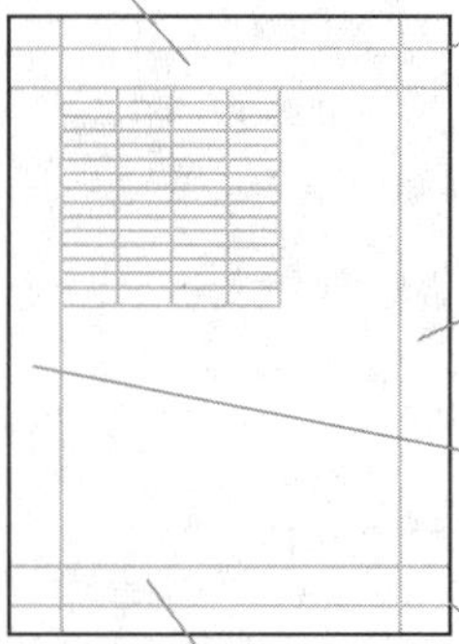

Using the Margins tab in the Page Setup dialog

Pull down the File menu and click Page Setup. Now carry out step 1 below, followed by steps 2-3 as appropriate. Finally, carry out step 4:

1 Ensure the Margins tab is active

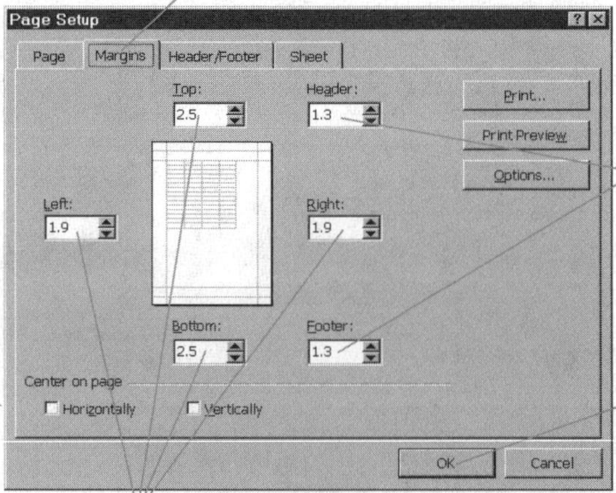

3 Type in header/footer settings

4 Click here

2 Type in the margin settings you need

HANDY TIP **To specify how your worksheet aligns on the page, click either option here:**

Setting header/footer options

Excel provides a list of built-in header and footer settings. You can apply any of these to the active worksheet. These settings include:

- the worksheet title
- the workbook title
- the date
- the user's name
- 'confidential'
- permutations of these

Using the Header/Footer tab in the Page Setup dialog

Pull down the File menu and click Page Setup. Now carry out step 1 below, followed by steps 2-3 as appropriate. Finally, carry out step 4:

1 Ensure the Header/Footer tab is active

2 Click here; select a header from the list

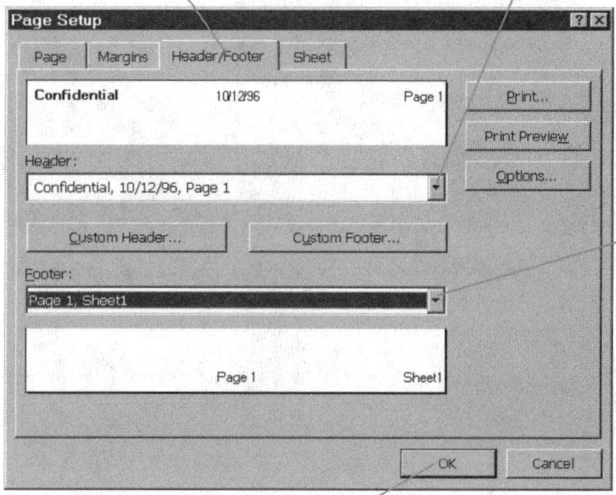

3 Click here; select a footer from the list

4 Click here

Setting sheet options

Excel lets you:

- define a printable area on-screen
- define a column or row title which will print on every page
- specify which worksheet components should print
- print with minimal formatting
- determine the print direction

HANDY TIP

If you want to print a specific cell range (area), type in the address here:

Using the Sheet tab in the Page Setup dialog

Pull down the File menu and click Page Setup. Now carry out step 1 below, followed by steps 2-4 (and the tips) as appropriate. Finally, carry out step 5.

1 Ensure the Sheet tab is active

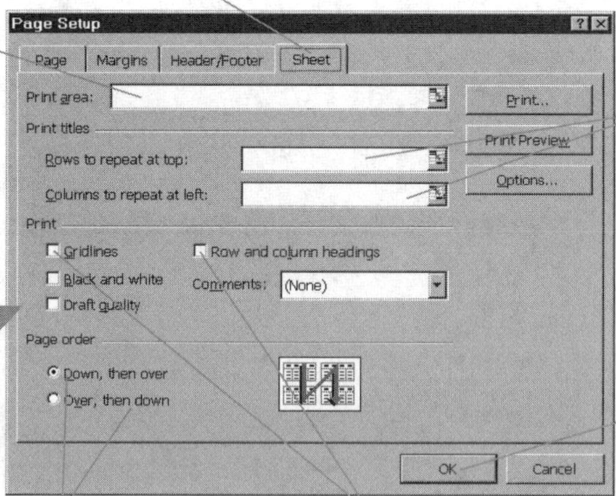

4 Type in the address of the row/column you want to use as a consistent title

5 Click here

HANDY TIP

Click Draft Quality for rapid printing with the minimum of formatting.

2 Click a direction option

3 Click a component to include or exclude it

Page setup for charts

Most page setup issues for charts in chart sheets are identical to those for worksheet data. The main difference, however, is that the Page Setup dialog has a Chart (rather than a Sheet) tab.

In the Chart tab, you can opt to have the chart

- printed at full size
- scaled to fit the page
- user-defined

You can also set the print quality.

Using the Chart tab in the Page Setup dialog

Click the relevant chart tab in the worksheet tab area. Pull down the File menu and click Page Setup. Now carry out step 1 below, followed by steps 2-3 as appropriate. Finally, carry out step 4.

HANDY TIP

Re step 3 – clicking Custom ensures that, when you return to the chart sheet, the chart size can be adjusted with the mouse in the normal way. The chart then prints at whatever size you set.

1 Ensure the Chart tab is active

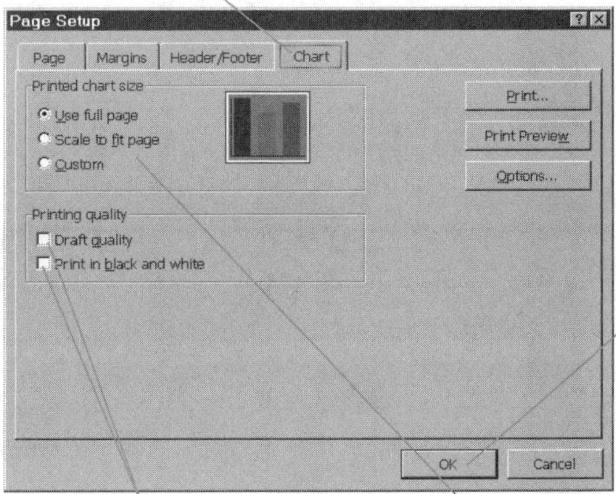

4 Click here

2 Click either option here to limit the print quality

3 Click any scale option here (see the tip)

Launching Print Preview

Excel provides a special view mode called Print Preview. This displays the active worksheet exactly as it will look when printed. Use Print Preview as a final check just before you begin printing.

You can perform the following actions from within Print Preview:

- moving from page to page
- zooming in or out on the active page
- adjusting most Page Setup settings
- adjusting margins visually

Excel's Print Preview mode has only two Zoom settings:

- Full Page
- High-Magnification

Launching Print Preview

Pull down the File menu and click Print Preview. This is the result:

To leave Print Preview mode and return to your worksheet (or chart sheet), simply press Esc.

Dedicated Print Preview toolbar

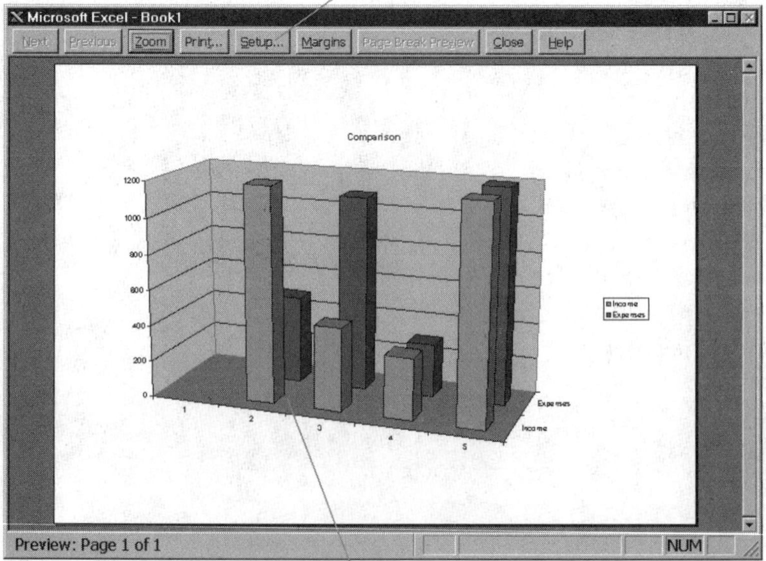

A preview of a chart sheet

Working with Print Preview

All of the operations you can perform in Print Preview mode can be accessed via the toolbar.

REMEMBER **Click the Page Break Preview button to launch this view – see page 110 for how to use it.**

HANDY TIP **Re step 6 – see earlier topics (pages 110-115) for how to use the Page Setup dialog.**

Using the Print Preview toolbar

Do any of the following, as appropriate:

1 Click here to jump to the next page

3 Click here to zoom in or out

6 Click here to launch the Page Setup dialog

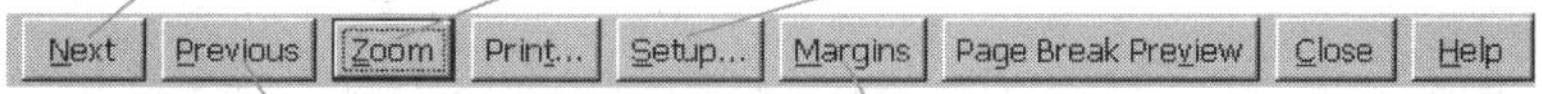

2 Click here to jump to the previous page

4 Click here to toggle margin markers on or off – then follow step 5

5 Drag any margin to reposition it (if margins are activated)

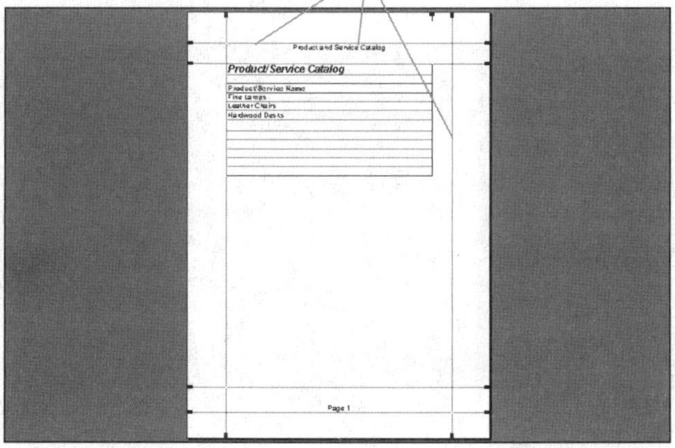

Printing worksheet data

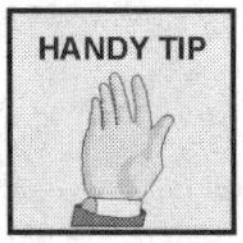

To begin printing at once (without launching the Print dialog), click this button:

in the Standard toolbar.

To select and print more than one worksheet, hold down Shift as you click on multiple tabs in the worksheet tab area.

If you need to adjust your printer's internal settings before you initiate printing, click Properties. Then refer to your printer's manual.

Excel lets you specify:

- the number of copies you want printed
- whether you want the copies 'collated'. This is the process whereby Excel prints one full copy at a time. For instance, if you're printing three copies of a 10-page worksheet, Excel prints pages 1-10 of the first copy, followed by pages 1-10 of the second and pages 1-10 of the third
- which pages (or page ranges) you want printed
- whether you want the print run restricted to cells you selected before initiating printing

You can 'mix and match' these, as appropriate.

Starting a print run

Open the workbook that contains the data you want to print. If you want to print an entire worksheet, click the relevant tab in the worksheet tab area. (Alternatively, if you need to print a specific cell range within a worksheet, select it.) Then pull down the File menu and click Print. Perform any of steps 1-5. Then carry out step 6 to begin printing.

1 Click here; select the printer you want from the list

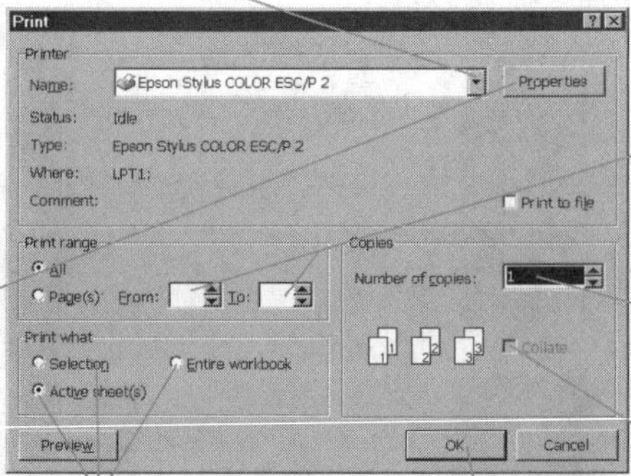

4 Type in a page range

3 Type in the number of copies required

2 Click the correct selection option

6 Click here

5 Click here to turn on collation

Chapter Four

Publisher

This chapter shows you how to use Publisher's Design Gallery to improve and enhance the impact of your documents. You'll also learn to achieve this by working directly with picture and text frames; in particular, you'll specify how the two components interact. Then you'll enter text and apply various formatting enhancements to it. Finally, you'll learn how to reset the page size/orientation; print your documents locally; and print to an outside service bureau.

Covers

The Design Gallery – an overview

REMEMBER

All Publisher wizards are highly customisable. For instance, you can specify whether you want pictures included.

REMEMBER

This is actually a series of 'grouped' objects.

Grouped objects are effectively treated as one, a technique which makes them easier to manipulate.

To group objects, hold down one Shift key as you select them. Then press Ctrl+Shift+G. (Repeat this keystroke combination to ungroup them.)

We saw in Chapter One how to create new Publisher documents with templates and wizards, and how to create new blank Publisher documents. We'll now explore how to work with existing documents to improve their layout. One principal way to do this is to use the Design Gallery.

The next illustration shows part of the Publisher screen:

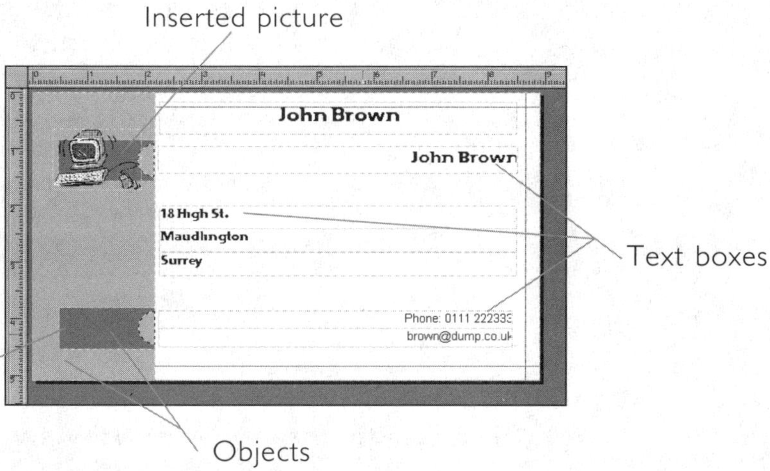

This is a business card, produced with the Business Card Wizard. Publisher has inserted:

- a picture
- a series of objects
- several text boxes

Although Publisher's wizards create attractive documents, you can use the Design Gallery to enhance them further. You can:

- add new graphical objects
- substitute a new object for any existing one
- apply a new format to an existing object
- store your own designs for future use

Using the Design Gallery (1)

Inserting new pictures

Refer to Publisher's vertical toolbar and do the following:

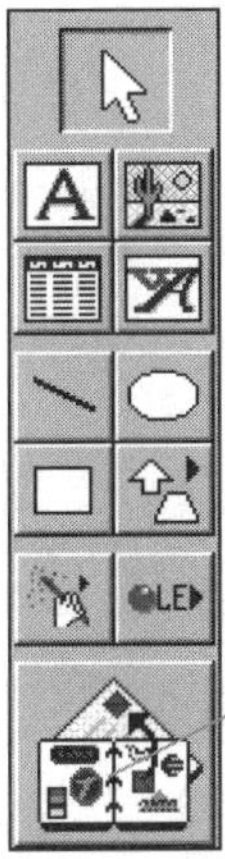

1 Click here

HANDY TIP **Re step 2 – the Design Gallery (a varied collection of design elements and pictures) organises its design elements under overall categories.**

HANDY TIP **If you want access to further categories/designs, click:**

More Designs

In the menu which launches, click the appropriate entry. Now follow steps 2 and 3.

HANDY TIP **When you've finished working with the Design Gallery, click here:**

Close

2 Select a category

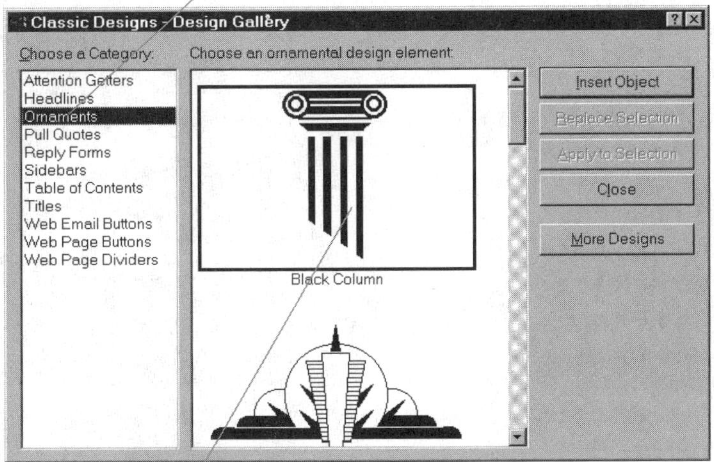

3 Double-click an image

Now use standard Windows techniques to resize/move the inserted picture, as appropriate.

Using the Design Gallery (2)

HANDY TIP **To store your own designs in the Design Gallery, click:**

In the menu, click Other Designs. Use the Other Designs dialog to locate the Publisher file which contains the relevant design elements. Double-click the file name.

HANDY TIP **If you want access to further categories/designs, click:**

In the menu which launches, click the appropriate entry. Now follow steps 2-4.

HANDY TIP **When you've finished working with the Design Gallery, click here:**

Replacing existing pictures

First, select the picture you want to replace. Then refer to Publisher's vertical toolbar and do the following:

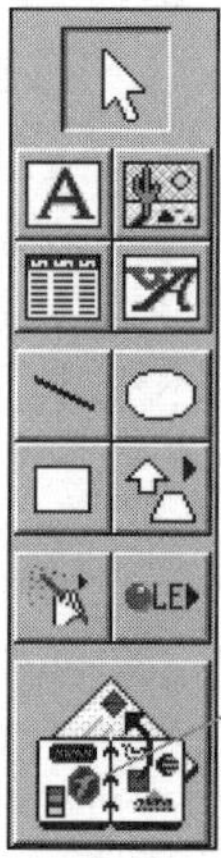

1 Click here

2 Select a category

4 Click here

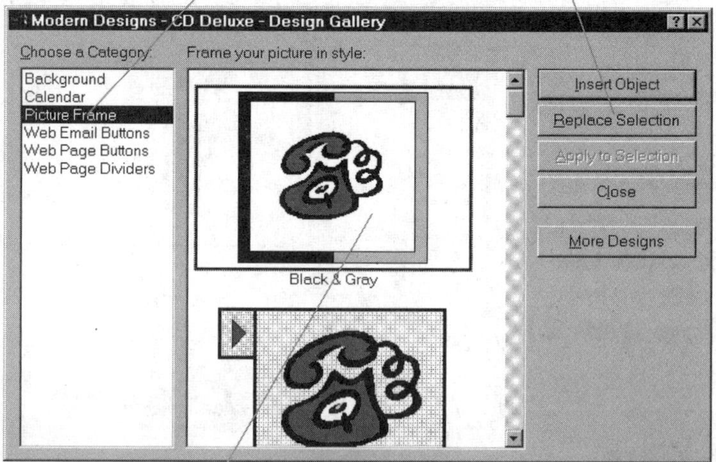

3 Select an image

Using the Design Gallery (3)

To insert a new page after the current one, press Ctrl+Shift+N.

You can only apply simple designs (consisting of one object) to existing objects.

If you want access to further categories/designs, click:

In the menu which launches, click the appropriate entry. Now follow steps 2 and 3.

When you've finished working with the Design Gallery, click here:

Applying new formats

First, select the picture you want to reformat. Then refer to Publisher's vertical toolbar and do the following:

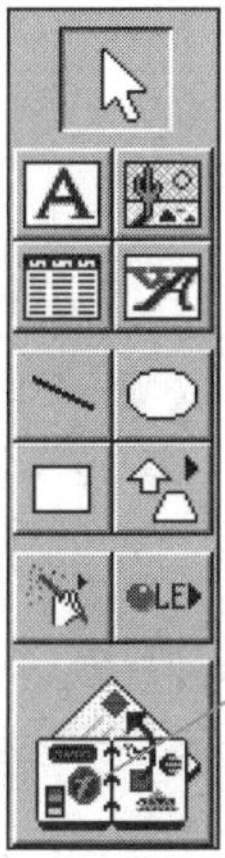

1 Click here

2 Select a category

4 Click here

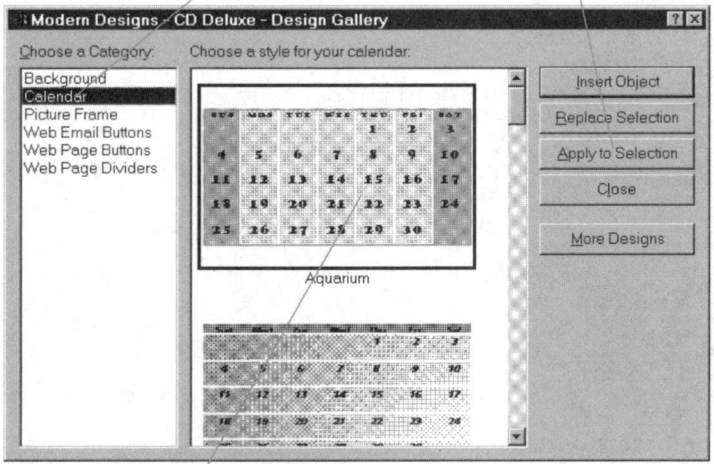

3 Select a design

Using frames (1)

HANDY TIP **Publisher surrounds frames with eight selection handles – see the illustration.**

HANDY TIP **To rescale a framed object, drag any of the handles outwards or inwards.**

To rescale a frame proportionately (i.e. without disrupting the height/width ratio), hold down Shift as you drag any of the corner handles.

HANDY TIP **You can use standard Windows techniques to move frames.**

In Publisher, all objects (including text) are contained in frames. Look at the next illustration:

Frames make it easier to format and manipulate design elements. You can:

- rescale frames
- move frames
- apply a border
- apply a fill
- crop frames (but not text frames)
- apply a shadow
- specify text wrap

Using frames (2)

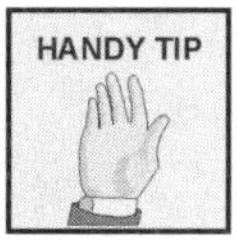

To select more than one frame, hold down Shift as you click them.

To crop a frame (i.e. reduce its size, thereby hiding part of the contents), first select it. Pull down the Format menu and click Crop Object. Move the mouse pointer over a handle – it changes to:

Drag the handle inwards.

An image before cropping...

And cropped from the right

Applying borders to frames

Select the frame(s) you want to border. Pull down the Format menu and click Border. Do the following:

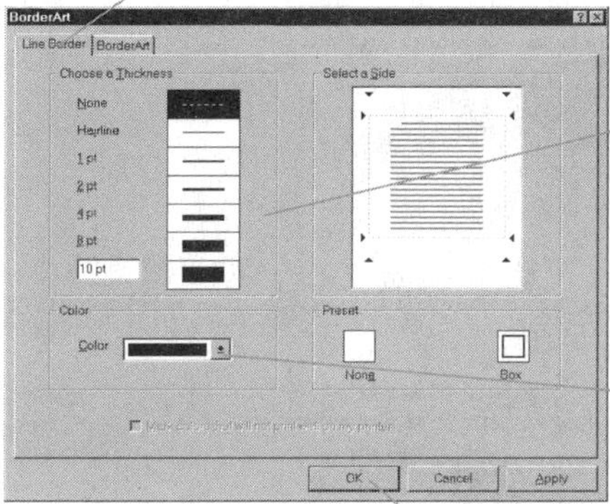

Applying fills to frames

Select the frame(s) you want to fill. Pull down the Format menu and click Fill Patterns and Shading. Do the following:

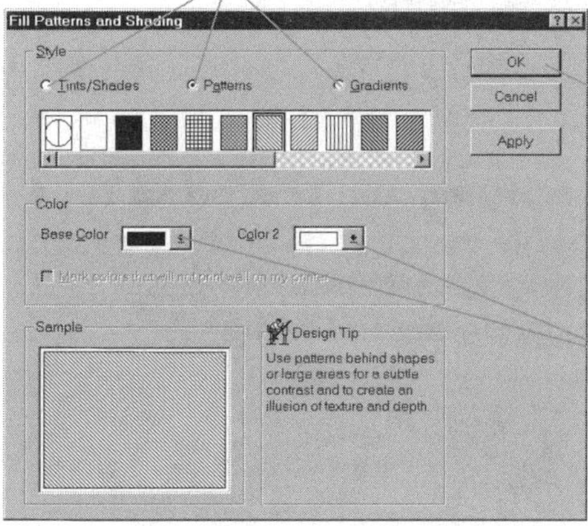

Using frames (3)

> **HANDY TIP**
>
> **To prevent any kind of text wrap, right-click the relevant *text* frame. In the menu which launches, select Text Frame Properties. In the Text Frame Properties dialog, deselect Wrap text around objects. Finally, click OK.**

Setting text wrap

It's important to specify how text in Publisher documents interacts with inserted pictures. There are three options:

- no text wrap (where text simply ignores the picture):

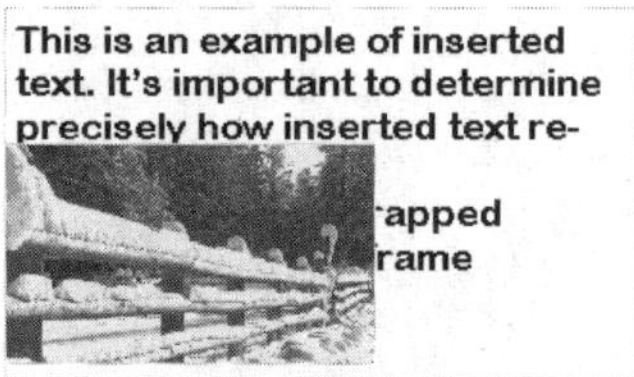

- text wrap around the enveloping frame:

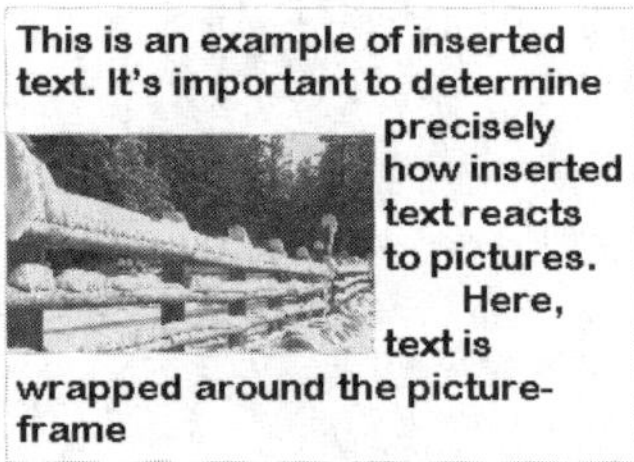

- text wrap around the picture within the frame:

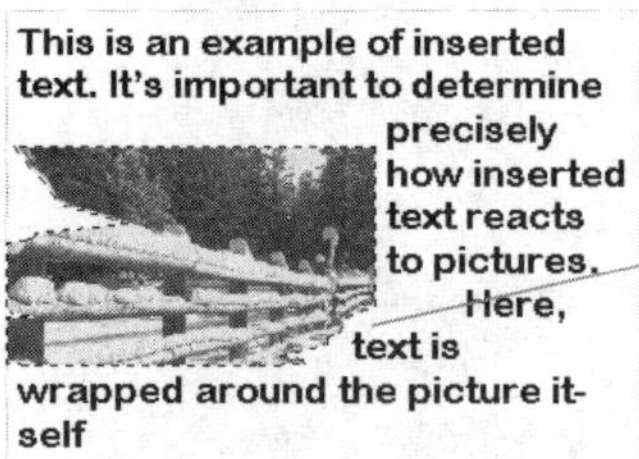

Text encroaches on the picture here

> **HANDY TIP**
>
> **To add shadow to a frame, select it then press Ctrl+D.**
>
> **The illustration below shows a shadowed picture:**

Specifying the text wrap type

Right-click the picture. In the menu which appears, click Picture Frame Properties. In the Picture Frame Properties dialog, do the following:

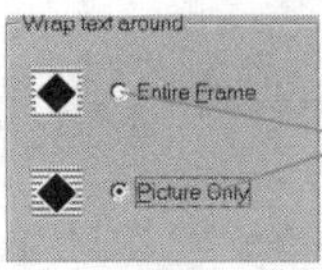

Click one of these

Finally, click OK.

Working with text (1)

Unlike Word, Publisher encloses text in a text frame. Doing so provides greater control and flexibility.

Entering text

Refer to the vertical toolbar and do the following:

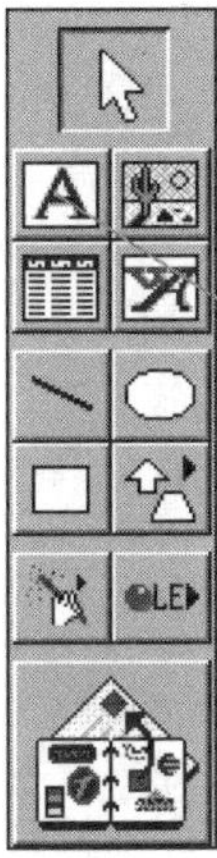

Now place the mouse pointer where you want the necessary text frame to begin. Drag the mouse diagonally to define it; release the mouse button to confirm creation of the frame. Begin entering text immediately:

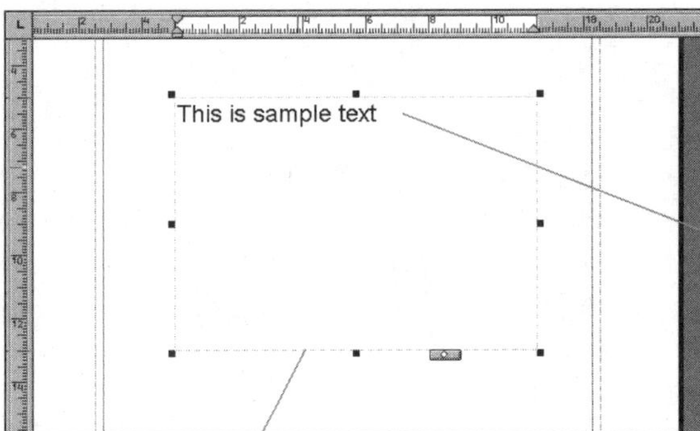

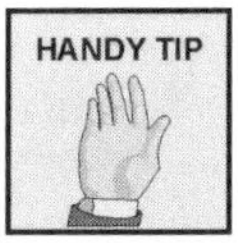

Text frames can be 'linked'. Linking ensures that text, when it exceeds the capacity of one frame, flows dynamically into the next.

Click the first frame. Click this button:

at the base of the frame. Now click in the second frame; Publisher re-flows the text accordingly.

Working with text (2)

You can format text in a variety of ways. You can apply:

- a typeface and/or type size
- a font style
- a font effect

Formatting text

Select the appropriate text. Pull down the Format menu and click Character. Carry out any of steps 1-4 below, then perform step 5:

1 Click here; select a font in the list

2 Type in a point size

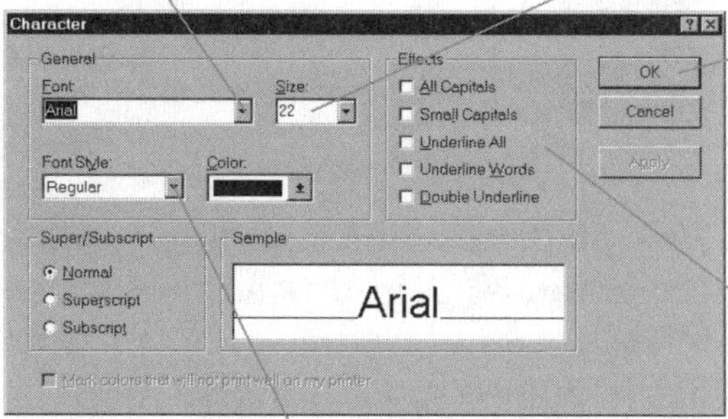

5 Click here

4 Select a font effect

3 Click here; select a font style (e.g. Bold) in the list

REMEMBER Text styles (as distinct from font styles – see step 3) are collections of text formatting.

By imposing a text style, you apply all of the associated formatting enhancements in one go. Using text styles can save you a lot of time and effort.

Applying a text style

Select the appropriate text. Refer to the Format toolbar (if it isn't on-screen, right-click the vertical toolbar and select Format Toolbar in the menu which appears). Do the following:

Click here; select a text style in the list

HANDY TIP To create a text style, format some sample text appropriately. Now click here:

Type in a name for the new style. Press Enter. In the Create Style By Example dialog, click OK.

Working with text (3)

HANDY TIP

Re step 1 – if you want to apply a bulleted or numbered list, click Bulleted List or Numbered List instead. The left-hand section of the dialog changes; complete the relevant fields. Finally, carry out step 4.

You can also specify:

- how text aligns with the left and right text margins
- an amount of line spacing

Aligning text

Select the appropriate text. Pull down the Format menu and click Indents and Lists. Do the following:

1 Ensure this is selected

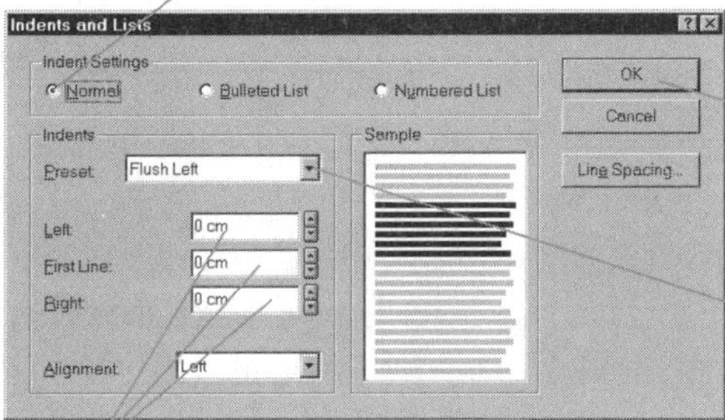

4 Click here

2 Click here; select an alignment from the list

3 Complete these, as necessary

REMEMBER

Line spacing is also known as leading (pronounced 'ledding').

HANDY TIP

Enter line and paragraph spacings in points.
72 points equate (roughly) to one inch.

Setting line spacing

Select the appropriate text. Pull down the Format menu and click Line Spacing. Do the following:

1 Type in a line spacing (e.g. '2sp' for double line spacing)

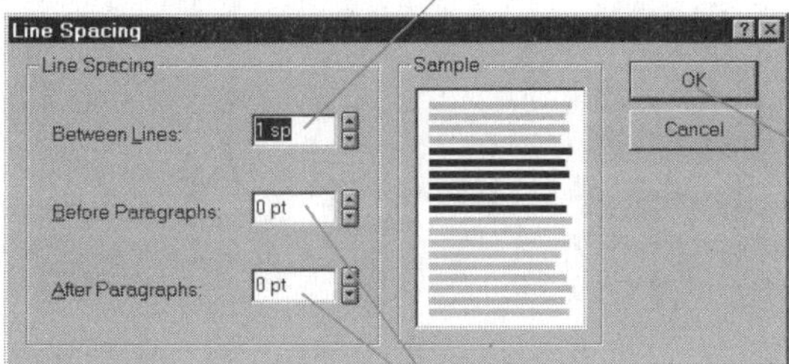

3 Click here

2 Optional – type in paragraph spacings

HANDY TIP

Re step 2 – the settings referred to here control the spacing before and after paragraphs.

Page setup

HANDY TIP

You can add headers or footers (text which appears respectively on the top or bottom of every page) to your documents.

Pull down the View menu and click Go To Background. Define a text frame in the appropriate location. Insert and format the relevant text. Finally, click Go To Foreground in the View menu.

By default, Publisher assumes that the active document's page size should be the same as the paper in your printer. However, you can change this if you need to (for instance, if you intend to print unusually sized documents such as business cards). You can also set the paper orientation. Available choices are:

Portrait

Landscape

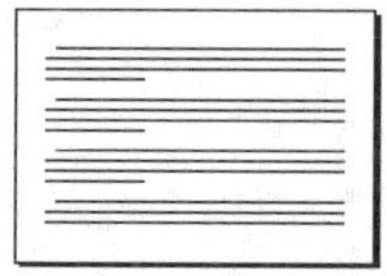

Specifying the page size/orientation

Pull down the File menu and click Page Setup. Carry out step 1 if you want your document's paper size to be the same as the printer's. Alternatively, carry out steps 2-3 to set a different size. Follow step 4 to apply an orientation. Finally, perform step 5:

HANDY TIP

Re step 3 – Publisher comes with a number of preset page sizes. However, if you want to define your own, click Custom in the list. Type in height and width details here:

Finally, carry out step 5.

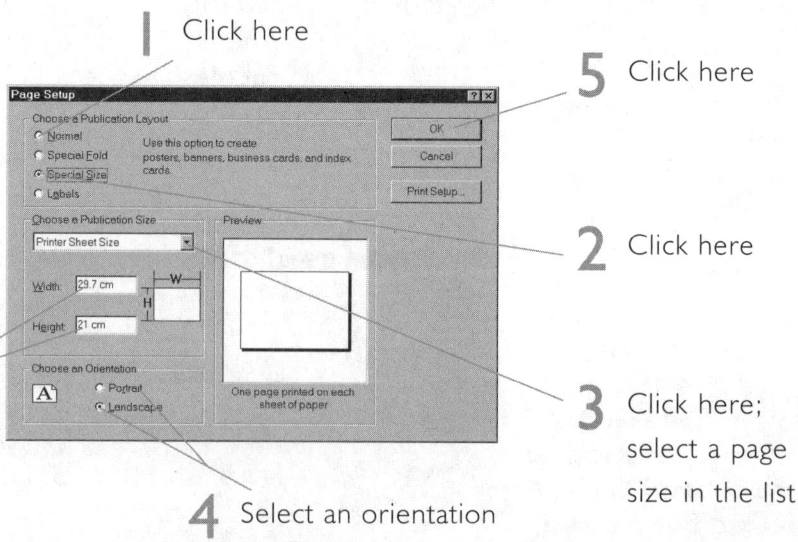

Local printing

Before you begin to print locally, you should ensure your printer's internal settings are correct.

Pull down the File menu and click Print Setup. Click this button:

in the Print Setup dialog. Complete the dialog that launches. (For how to do this, consult your printer's manual.) Click OK twice.

Ensure this is selected to have Publisher troubleshoot your print jobs to make sure errors aren't perpetuated.

Re step 3 – for a definition of collation, see page 75.

Publisher recognises two basic printing needs:

- printing to a printer (usually an inkjet or laser) attached to your PC
- printing to an outside service bureau

The second method is more complex, and involves translating your work into a special file and submitting this on disk to a bureau or copy shop. Fortunately, Publisher makes this process remarkably straightforward.

To begin local printing, pull down the File menu and click Print. Now carry out any of steps 1-4, as appropriate. Finally, perform step 5:

1 Click here; select a printer in the list

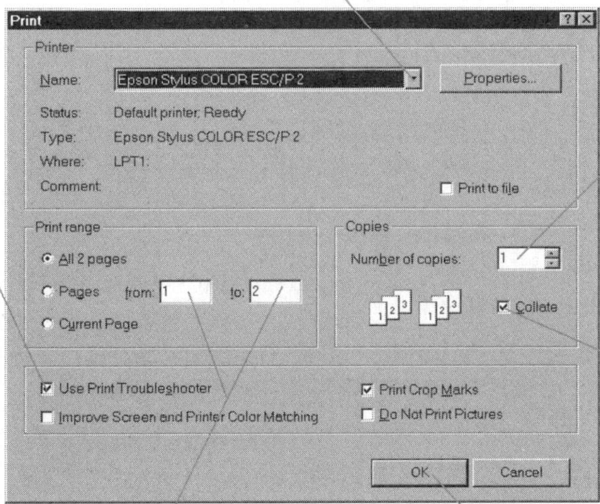

2 Type in the no. of copies required

3 Click here to deselect collation

4 Type in start and end page numbers

5 Click here

Outside printing

REMEMBER

There is also a third, optional stage: printing a proof copy.

Before you send your completed file to the relevant bureau, follow steps 1-5. In step 4, though, *deselect* Print to file. Publisher prints a draft copy on your local printer.

REMEMBER

After step 5, the Print To File dialog appears. Select the drive/folder where you want the print file stored. Name the file in the File name field. Click OK. Now transfer the file to one or more floppy disks and take (or e-mail) it to the bureau.

HANDY TIP

Some bureaus will accept files in Publisher's own (.PUB) format.

There are two stages to outside printing. First, you run a specific setup procedure, then you produce the necessary file (usually a .PRN file, but see the Handy Tip below).

Outside setup

Pull down the File menu and click Outside Print Setup. Do the following:

1 Click one of these

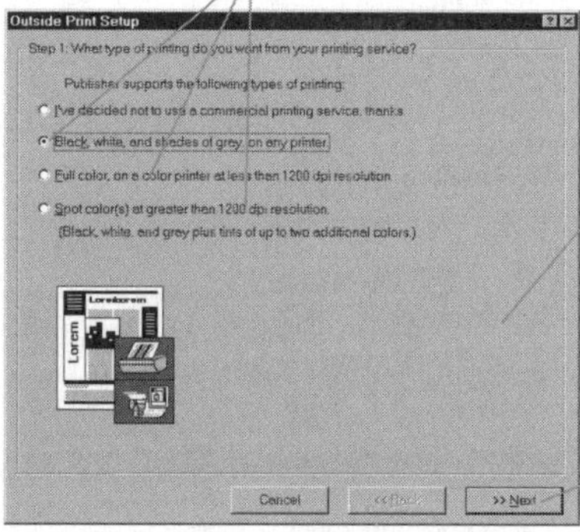

2 Further options appear here if you're printing spot colours – complete them as necessary

3 Click here

Publisher now launches two additional dialogs. Complete these appropriately, then click Done.

Outside printing

Pull down the File menu and click Print to Outside Printer. Do the following:

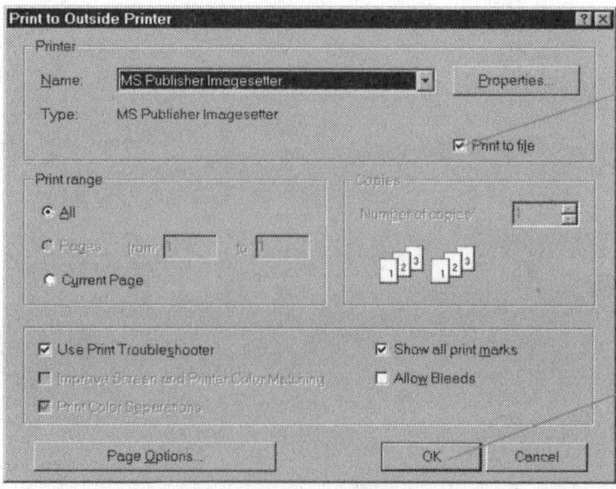

4 Ensure this is selected

5 Click here

Chapter Five

AutoRoute Express

This chapter shows you how to use the AutoRoute Express Home screen as a springboard. You'll view the underlying map, customising how much detail displays, then zoom in on specific map areas. Then you'll learn how to locate and view specific locations, and how to view the illustrative photographs supplied with AutoRoute Express. Finally, you'll have AutoRoute Express calculate the best route between two locations (taking into account an intervening stop, if required, and also specifying which associated features you want included), and connect to World Wide Web sites which offer supplementary information on specific locations.

Covers

The Home screen

REMEMBER

Because AutoRoute Express is so different to the other Office modules, this chapter will explore its screens in some detail.

HANDY TIP

Just after you've calculated a route, you can save the details to disk for future use.

Press Ctrl+S. The Save As dialog launches. Use the Save in field to choose a host drive/ folder; name the route in the File name field. Click Save.

HANDY TIP

To open a saved route, press Ctrl+O. Use the Open dialog to locate the route drive/folder; type in the route name in the File name field. Click Open.

When you start AutoRoute Express, the following screen appears:

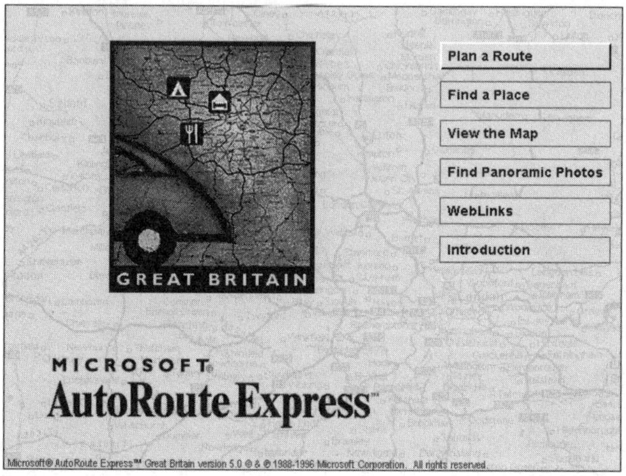

The Home screen

This is the AutoRoute Express Home screen. The Home screen is the launch-pad from which the following actions are initiated:

- dynamic viewing of the underlying map
- locating places and sites
- viewing photographs
- route planning
- connecting to special sites on the World Wide Web for additional information about map locations. These sites contain a wealth of information aimed at tourists and visitors.

  N.B. To connect to these sites, you need:

  — an Internet browser
  — a modem
  — a valid, live Internet connection

Viewing the map (1)

To view the AutoRoute Express map, do the following in the Home screen:

Click here

This is the result:

Menu bar

The Map screen

Dedicated toolbar

Scale

REMEMBER **You can specify the type of map display. Right-click anywhere in the map. In the menu, click Map Display. In the Map Display dialog, ensure the Map Styles tab is active. Select any of the following:**

- Detailed terrain view (provides maximum detail)
- Terrain view (less geographic detail)
- Detailed road map view (emphasises road detail)
- Road map view (road detail with fewer geographic features)

Finally, click OK.

Viewing the map (2)

To print a map, press Ctrl+P. Complete the Print dialog appropriately. Click Print.

Once you've displayed the map, you can use the following techniques to zoom in on (magnify) the area you're interested in:

Selective zooming

To view a specific section of the map in more detail, refer to the toolbar and do the following:

Click here

Now move the mouse cursor (an arrow over a dotted box) over the relevant Map section and click once. AutoRoute Express produces a context-sensitive menu. Do the following:

Click a location

When you've zoomed in on the map, you can move the visible component.
Click this button:

in the toolbar. Place the mouse pointer over the map; hold down the left mouse button and drag the map until the correct component displays. Release the button.

Using the Zoom slider

To view the map in more detail, refer to the toolbar and do the following:

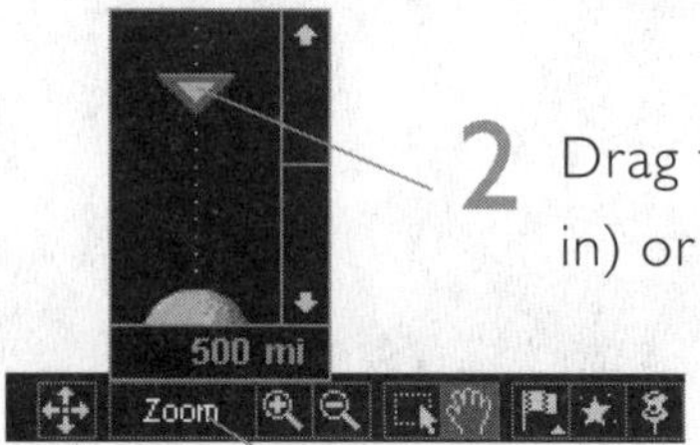

2 Drag this down (to zoom in) or up (to zoom out)

1 Click here

Locating places

Do the following from within the AutoRoute Express Home screen:

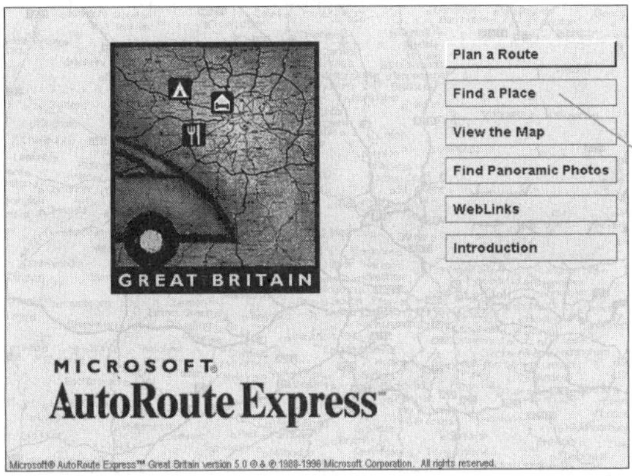

Click here

Now carry out the following steps:

1 Type in a place name

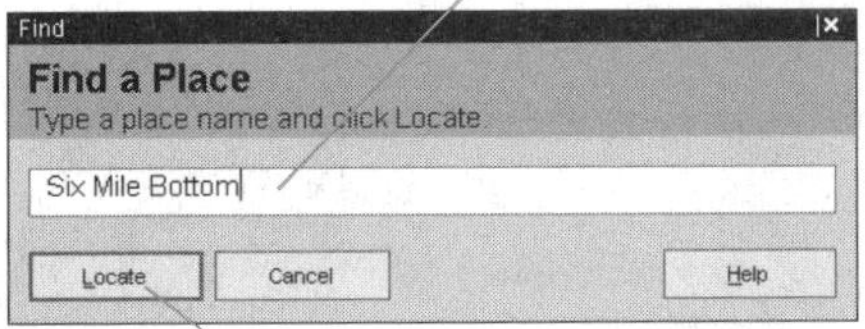

2 Click here

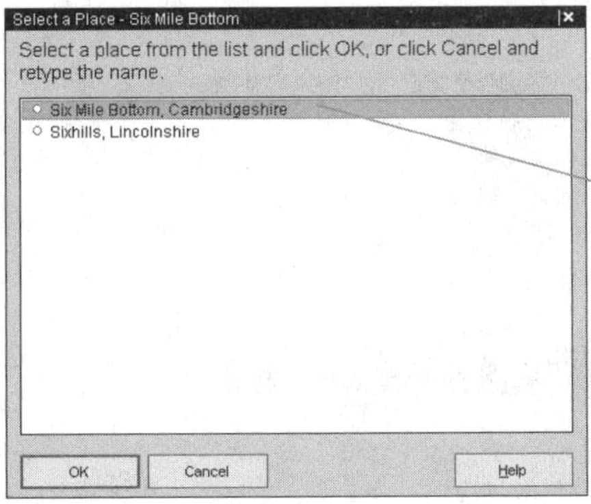

3 Double-click the correct location

HANDY TIP You can also launch the Find dialog from within the Map screen. Simply press Ctrl+G.

HANDY TIP Re step 1 – to locate pushpins, type in the pushpin name. (See page 139 for how to insert pushpins.)

REMEMBER After step 3, AutoRoute Express launches a magnified view of the map centred on the specified location.

Viewing photographs (1)

AutoRoute Express comes with numerous photographs (some of them panoramic, i.e. covering 360°) which illustrate locations and sites.

Viewing panoramic photographs

Do the following within the Home screen:

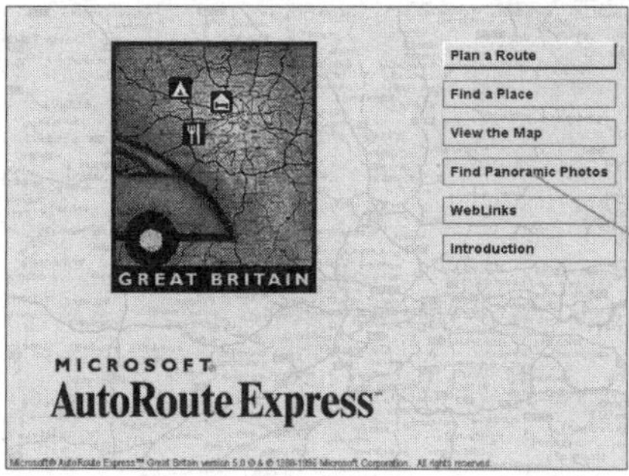

1 Click here

HANDY TIP **You can launch this dialog within the Map screen.**

Pull down the Find menu and click 360° Views.

Now carry out the following action:

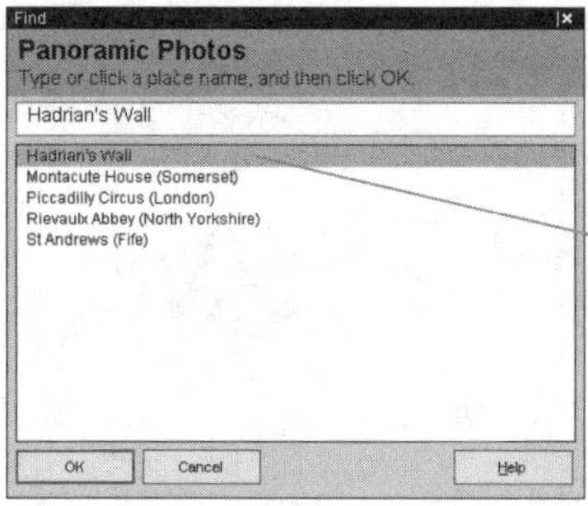

2 Double-click a photograph

HANDY TIP **AutoRoute Express pans the photograph over 360°. To return to the Home screen when you've finished viewing it, click this button:**

Home

in the Menu bar.

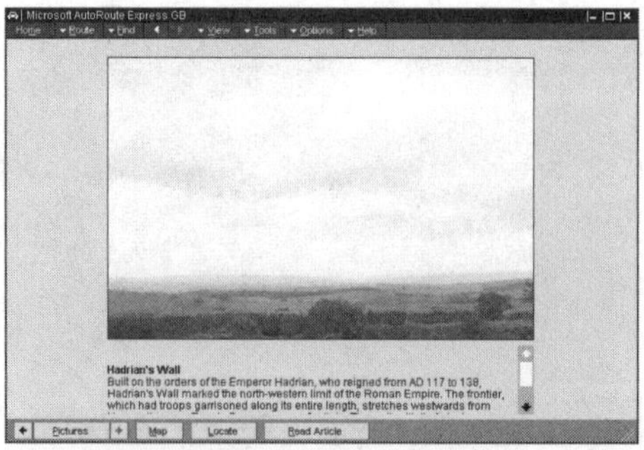

A panoramic photograph

Viewing photographs (2)

Viewing static photographs

Do the following within the Map screen:

1 Click here

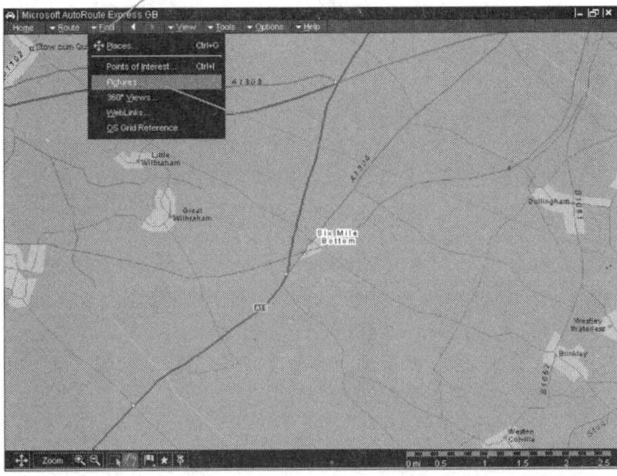

2 Click here

Now carry out the following action:

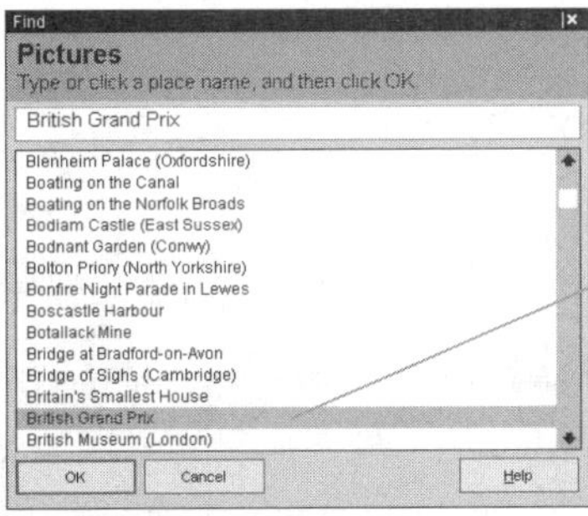

3 Double-click a photograph

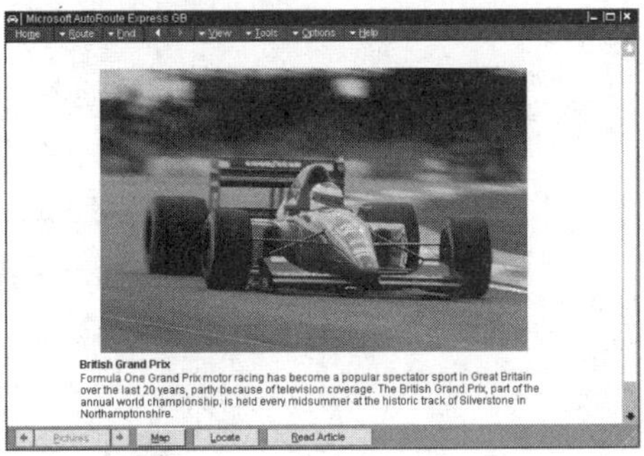

A photograph

HANDY TIP You can insert your own markers – 'pushpins' – into maps.

Click this button in the toolbar:

Move the mouse pointer over the relevant map area and click once. Complete the Pushpin Properties dialog. (Note that pushpin names should have at least 3 characters.) Click OK.

HANDY TIP See page 137 for how to search for inserted pushpins.

HANDY TIP To return to the Home screen when you've finished viewing it, click this button:

Home

in the Menu bar.

Route planning (1)

You can have AutoRoute Express calculate a route based on:

- the start and destination
- (optional) a stopover location en route
- specified features en route (e.g. accommodation or restaurants)

Planning a route

Do the following within the Home screen:

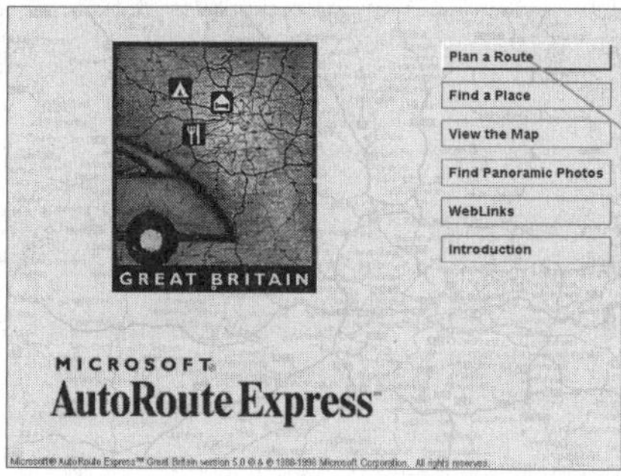

Click here

Now carry out the following steps:

1 Type in the start location; press Enter

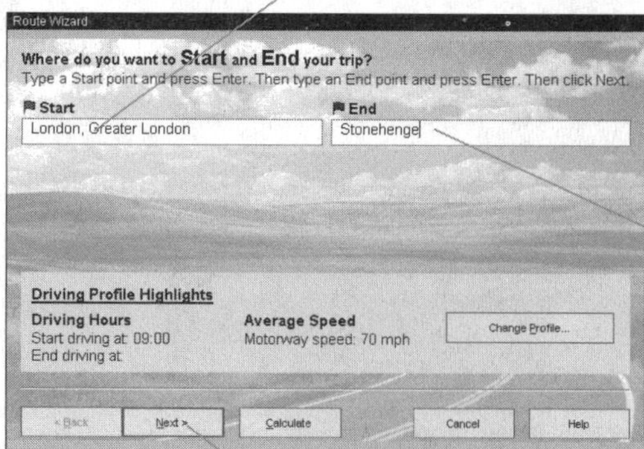

2 Type in the destination; press Enter

3 Click here

HANDY TIP **You can also export routes. Press Ctrl+C. In the dialog which launches, do the following:**

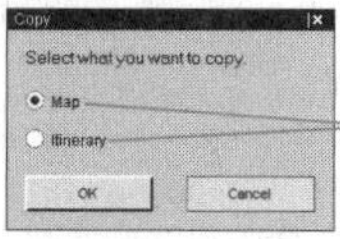

Click one of these

Then click OK. In Word or Publisher, press Ctrl+V to paste in the route.

HANDY TIP **To initiate the route planning process from the Map screen, press Ctrl+R.**

REMEMBER **After steps 1 and 2, this dialog launches:**

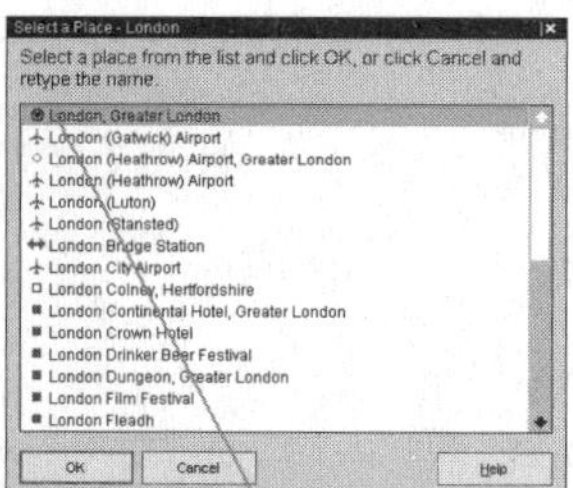

Double-click the correct definition

Route planning (2)

After step 1, this dialog launches:

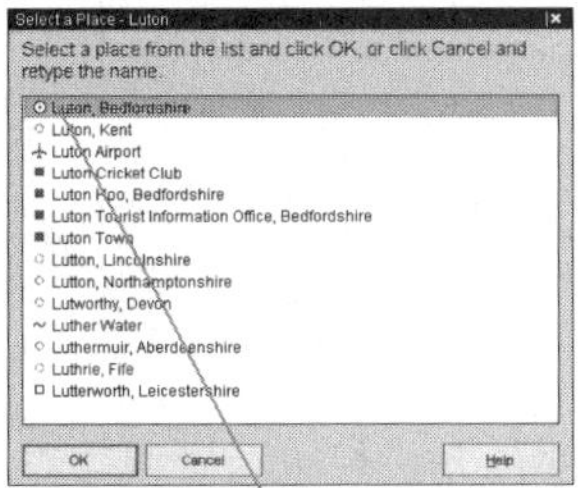

Double-click the correct definition

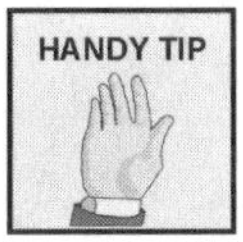

Step 3 sets the distance from the route within which features are shown.

After step 6, AutoRoute Express calculates the route, then launches a summation dialog. Click OK to view the completed route:

Now perform the following steps:

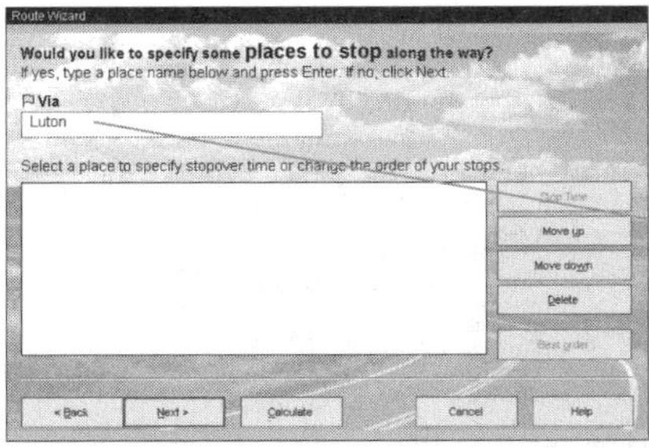

1 Optional – enter an intermediate stop and press Enter

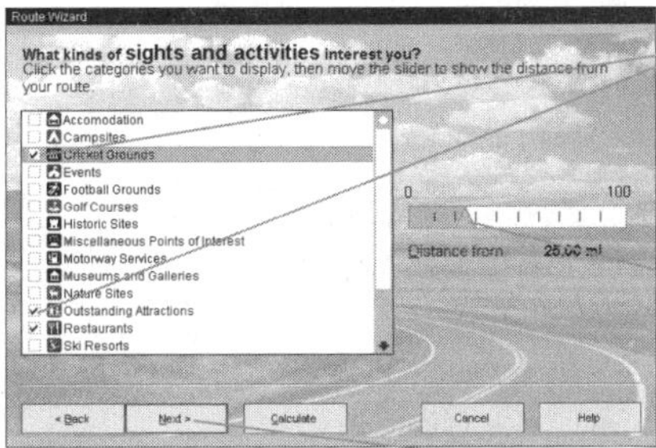

2 Select one or more features you want the route to display

3 Click a defining distance

4 Click here

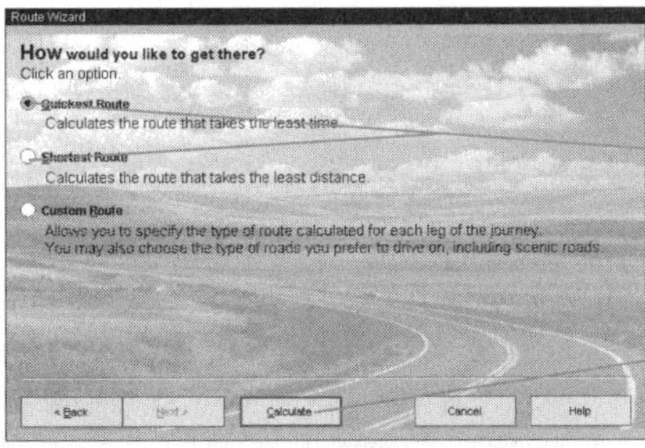

5 Select a calculation method

6 Click here

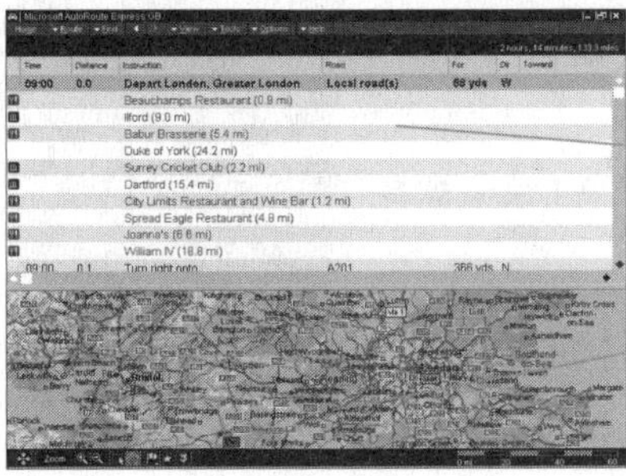

The printed itinerary

The mapped route

Using WebLinks

From within AutoRoute Express, you can link directly to World Wide Web sites which offer information specific to given locations.

Do the following within the Home screen:

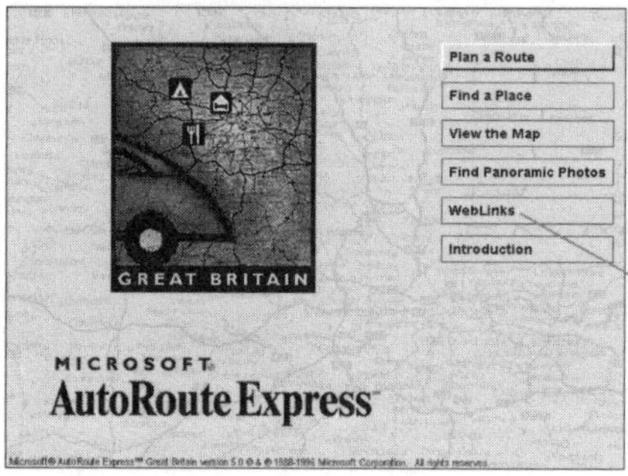

1 Click here

Now carry out the following steps:

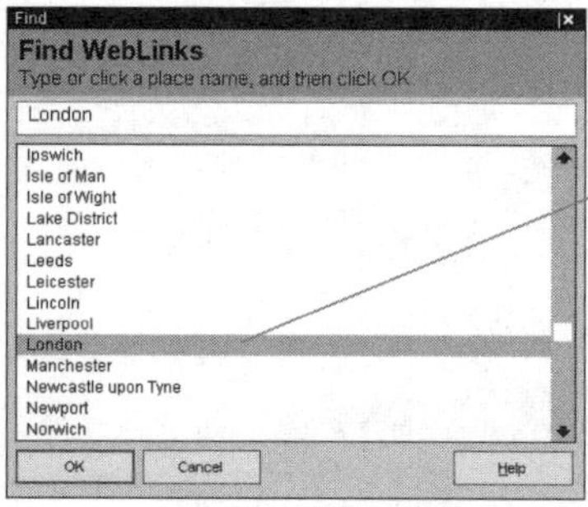

2 Double-click a place name

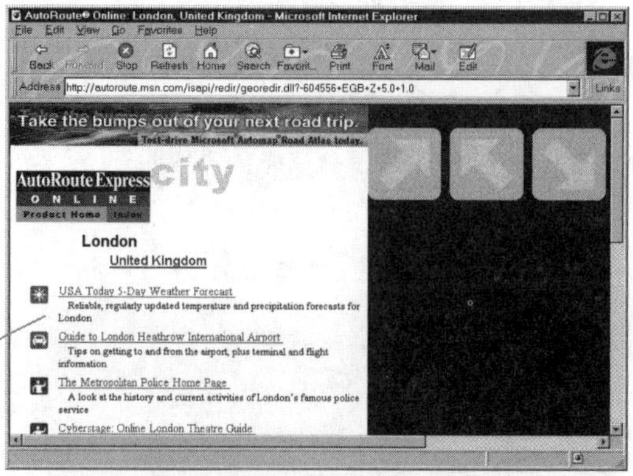

The AutoRoute Express site for London

To connect to the Web, you need:

- a modem
- a live Internet connection
- an active browser

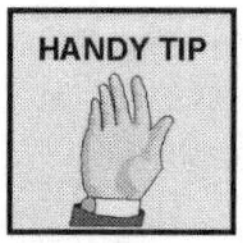

To print a route, press Ctrl+P. Three successive Print dialogs launch; complete these appropriately. Finally, click Finish to begin printing.

After step 2, AutoRoute Express launches a confirmatory dialog. Do the following:

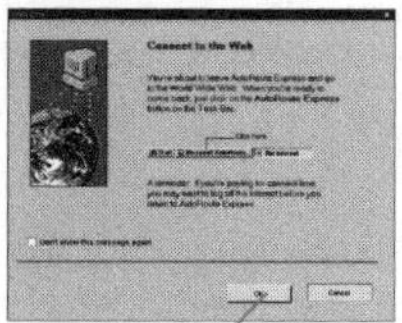

Click here

The specified site is now displayed in your browser:

Chapter Six

Outlook

This chapter provides a brief introduction to the *stand-alone* (i.e. non-workgroup) use of Outlook. Use it to learn how to use the Outlook bar to launch any of Outlook's associated folders. You'll enter appointments/events, tasks and contact details; Outlook will then coordinate them so that you can manage your business/personal affairs more easily. You'll also set up and use Outlook to transmit and receive e-mail, using – if you want – Microsoft Word as your editor.

Covers

The Outlook screen

The Folder banner tells you which Outlook folder (in this case, Inbox – see page 145) is active.

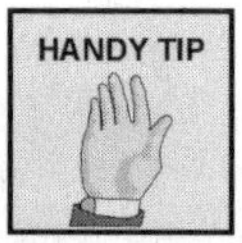

To print out work you do in any component on the Outlook bar, first click the relevant folder. Press Ctrl+P. Complete the Print dialog as normal. In particular, select a print style (the choices vary with the folder selected). Finally, click OK to begin printing.

Below is a detailed illustration of a typical Outlook screen.

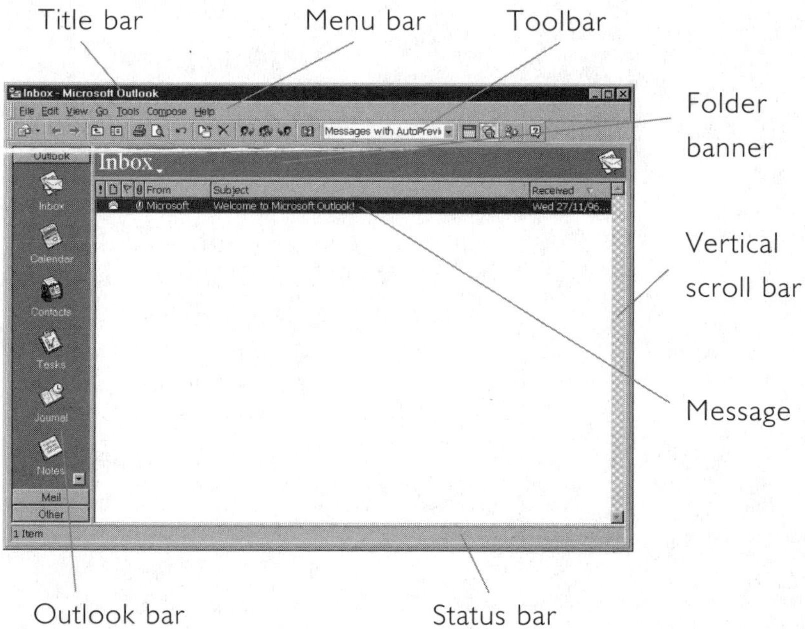

Some of these – e.g. the menu and scroll bars – are standard to just about all programs that run under Windows. However, you can specify which of the two available toolbars display.

Specifying which toolbars display

Pull down the View menu and do the following:

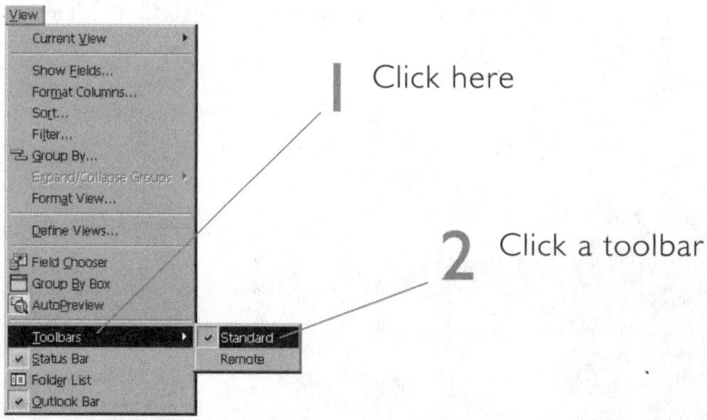

Using the Outlook bar

REMEMBER

Outlook organises its features into folders. All folders are accessible from the Outlook bar.

HANDY TIP

To insert a note, click the Notes folder in the Outlook bar. Press Ctrl+N. Do the following:

Type in your note, then press Alt+F4

When you run Outlook, it automatically opens the Inbox. This is the Outlook folder in which incoming messages are stored. However, there are several additional folders you can access. These include:

Calendar	A tool to help you schedule events, tasks, appointments and meetings
Contacts	A tool to help you manage business/ personal contacts
Tasks	A task management aid
Notes	Acts as a jotting pad; you can create 'sticky' notes
Mail	Includes Inbox, and also these folders:

— Sent Items

— Outbox

— Deleted items

Activating folders

Do the following:

Click a folder icon

REMEMBER

Click Mail for access to additional delivery-based features.

REMEMBER

Click Other for access to standard folders, e.g. My Computer.

Working with the Calendar (1)

HANDY TIP

Outlook has another folder which you can use to oversee your schedule: Journal. You can have Journal record messages, meetings and task requests automatically. It will also record Office documents.

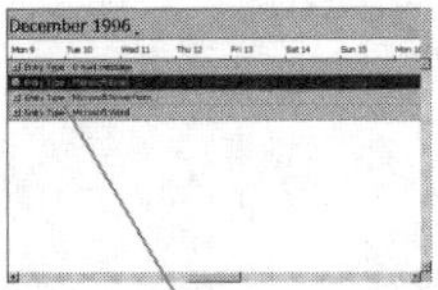

Auto-recorded entries

To specify what is recorded in Journal, click the Journal icon in the Outlook bar. Click Options in the Tools menu. In the Journal tab, make the relevant selections. Click OK.

REMEMBER

See page 144 for how to make the Standard toolbar visible.

The Calendar provides alternative ways of viewing and interacting with your schedules. The main views are:

Day/Week/Month	The all-purpose view. An aspect of the Appointment Book; used to enter appointments, events and tasks. You can specify whether you work in the Day, Week or Month aspects. (See below.)
Active Appointments	An aspect of the Appointment Book; used to enter and monitor active appointments.
Events	An aspect of the Appointment Book, useful for entering and monitoring events.

Some aspects of Outlook – for instance, the use of the Calendar to coordinate meetings among workgroup members – are beyond the scope of this book.

Switching between the Day, Week and Month Calendars

You'll probably use Day/Week/Month view more than any other, because it offers great flexibility. By default, the Calendar displays appointments etc. with the use of the Day aspect. To change the aspect, refer to the Standard toolbar and click any of the following:

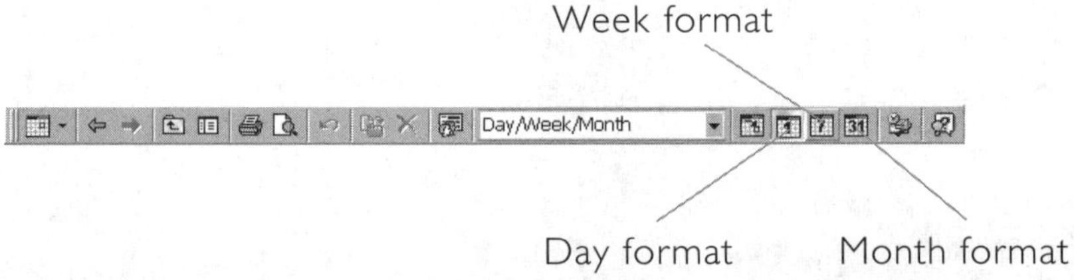

Working with the Calendar (2)

Re step 2 – if the date shown in the Date Navigator isn't correct, click the following:

◄ or ►

to go back or forward by one month respectively.

If you need to designate an appointment as recurring, carry out steps 1-3. Then double-click the appointment. In the toolbar within the dialog which launches, click this button:

In the Appointment Recurrence dialog, set the relevant options. Click OK. Now click the following:

You can add appointments to the Daily Calendar.

If you want, you can stipulate that the appointment is recurring (i.e. it's automatically entered at an interval you specify).

Adding an appointment in the Daily Calendar

Carry out steps 1, 2 and 3 below (then follow the procedures in the Remember tip if you want to mark the appointment as recurring):

2 Click the correct day

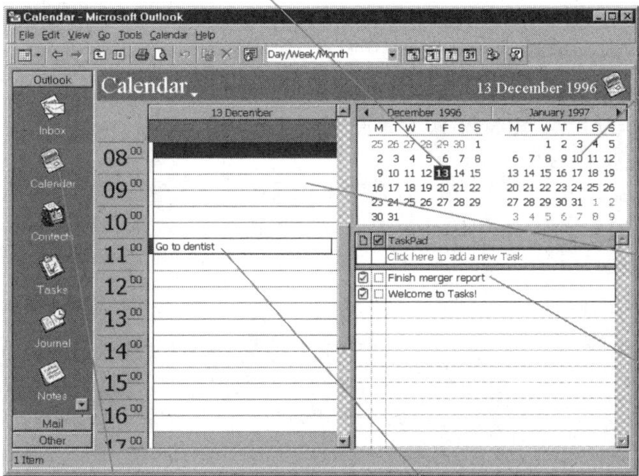

Date Navigator

Appointment Book

TaskPad

1 Ensure the Calendar folder is active

3 Click the relevant time slot; then type in details of the appointment and press Return

Outlook adds the new appointment to the Calendar.

Working with the Calendar (3)

You can add events to the Daily Calendar.

Outlook handles events in a rather different way to appointments. For example, they don't occupy specific time slots in your Appointment Book. Instead, they can relate to any day and can even extend over more than one.

Outlook distinguishes between events and annual events. Annual events occur yearly on a specific date.

Examples of events include:

- birthdays and anniversaries
- shows
- seminars

REMEMBER

If you need to amend or update an existing event, double-click its button within the Appointment Book. Then follow steps 1-3 here, as appropriate.

Events display as buttons within the Appointment Book.

Adding an event to the Daily Calendar

Right-click the relevant date/time slot. In the menu, click New Event. Now do the following:

REMEMBER

Re step 1 – to insert an *annual* event, instead of a start and end date, simply type in the date on which you want the annual event to recur.

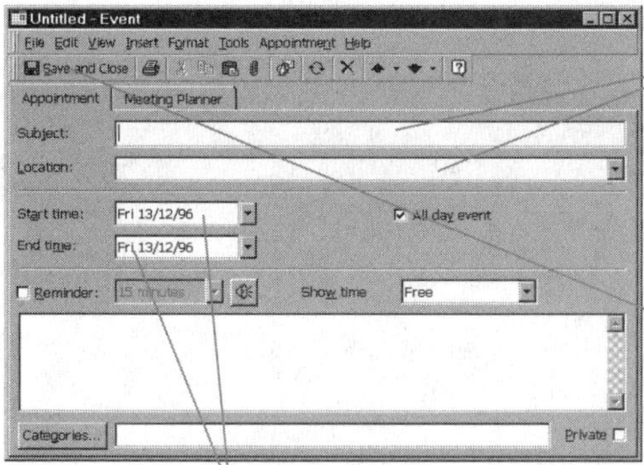

2 Enter a description

3 Click here

1 Type in start and end dates

To mark an event as recurring, carry out steps 1-3 above. Then double-click the event in the Appointment Book. Now follow the procedures set out in the Remember tip on page 147.

Working with the Calendar (4)

Use the Weekly view as an alternative way to display your appointments and events.

In the Weekly Calendar, you can enter appointments and events in the same way that you can in the Daily Calendar – see 'Working with the Calendar (1)' and 'Working with the Calendar (2)' for how to do this.

Moving around in the Weekly Calendar

You can jump to a specific date in the Weekly Calendar. To do this, pull down the Go menu and click Go to Date. Carry out steps 1-4 and 7:

You can also use the Go To Date dialog (from within any Calendar view) to switch between the Day, Week and Month Calendars. Follow steps 5-7.

1 Click here

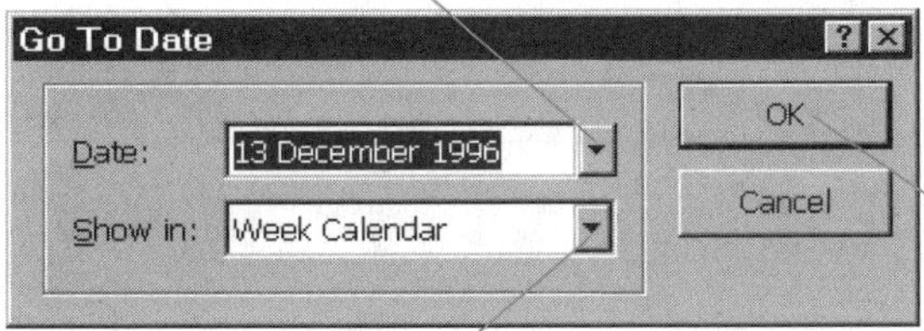

7 Click here

5 Click here

2 (Optional) Click here to move one month back

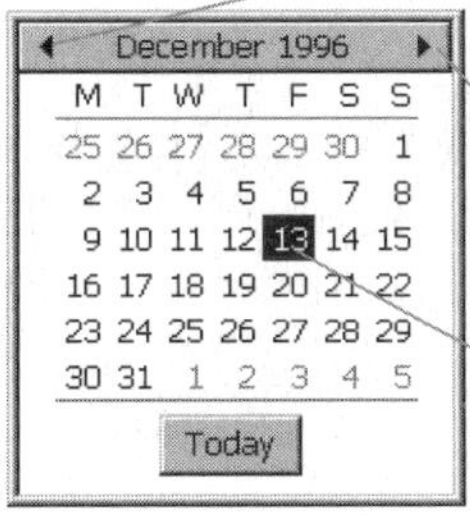

3 (Optional) Click here to move one month forward

4 Click the day you want to view

6 Select the Calendar view

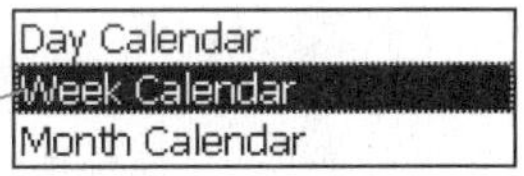

Working with the Calendar (5)

Use the Monthly Calendar to gain a useful overview of your schedule.

It's not a good idea, however, to use it to insert appointments directly; you can do so, but you may well find that the scale is too small to make the process convenient. Instead, use the following method.

Inserting a new appointment in the Monthly Calendar

Right click in the Calendar. In the menu which launches, click New Appointment. Then carry out steps 1-3 below:

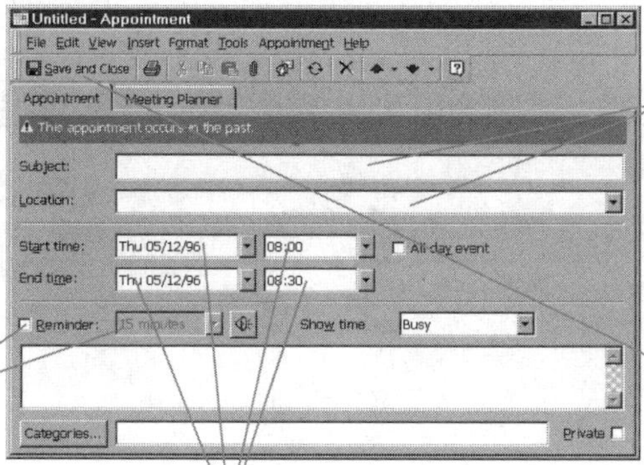

HANDY TIP

Click Reminder (then insert a reminder interval) if you want Outlook to prompt you when an appointment is due.

Inserting a new event in the Monthly Calendar

You can insert events in the Monthly Calendar by using the same techniques as for the Daily Calendar. See the 'Working with the Calendar (3)' topic earlier.

Working with the Tasks folder

Use the Tasks folder to enter and track tasks.

When you've entered a task into the Tasks folder, it displays in the TaskPad in the Daily and Weekly Calendars.

HANDY TIP

If you need to amend or update an existing task, click within it and follow steps 1 and 2.

HANDY TIP

Various views are available in the Tasks folder. To switch between views, click Current View in the View menu; select a view in the sub-menu.

Entering a task

If the Tasks folder isn't already active, click the Tasks icon in the Outlook bar. Then do the following:

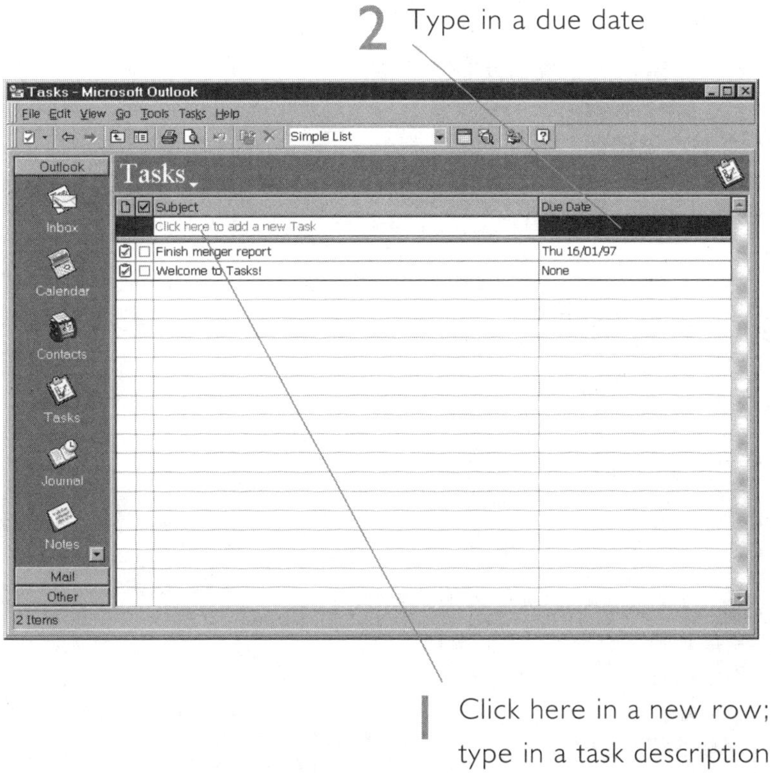

REMEMBER

Tasks can be prioritised. Outlook recognises three levels: Low, Normal and High.

Customising tasks

The above steps produce a basic task. If you want to customise the settings in more depth (for instance, you can set start and end dates, reminder intervals and/or priority levels), double-click the task. Complete the dialog which launches, then click Save and Close.

Working with the Contacts folder

HANDY TIP **Another view – Detailed Address Cards – uses the card model but with even more detail...**

HANDY TIP **To switch between views, click Current View in the View menu; select a view in the sub-menu.**

Use the Contacts folder as a convenient place to keep track of business/personal contacts.

Outlook displays contacts in various forms. The following models are used:

- a grid (e.g. Phone List view)
- a business card model (e.g. Address Cards view)

You can enter contacts directly into both contact types, but you may find that the card-based views make the job easier.

Entering a contact

If the Contacts view isn't already active, click the Contacts icon in the Outlook bar. Then do the following:

HANDY TIP **If you need to amend a contact, double-click it. Then carry out steps 3-4 as appropriate.**

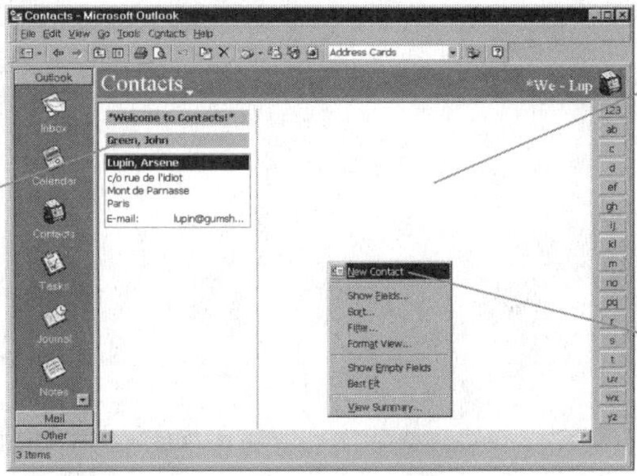

1 Right-click anywhere here

2 Click here

HANDY TIP **To set advanced contact details, click any of the tabs here:**

Complete the relevant fields, then carry out step 4.

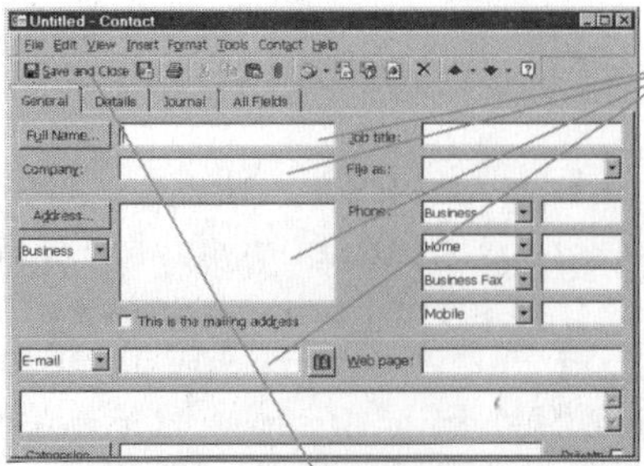

3 Enter contact details

4 Click here

Selecting an information service

A user profile consists of settings which define how Outlook operates. It determines (among other things) how Outlook sends and receives mail via one or more associated information services.

You can use Outlook to send and receive e-mail. Before you can do this, however, you need to:

- install an information service (if necessary)
- add it to your user profile

Several information services (e.g. Internet Mail) are automatically installed with Outlook.

Adding an information service

Pull down the Tools menu and click Services. Now carry out steps 1-3 below:

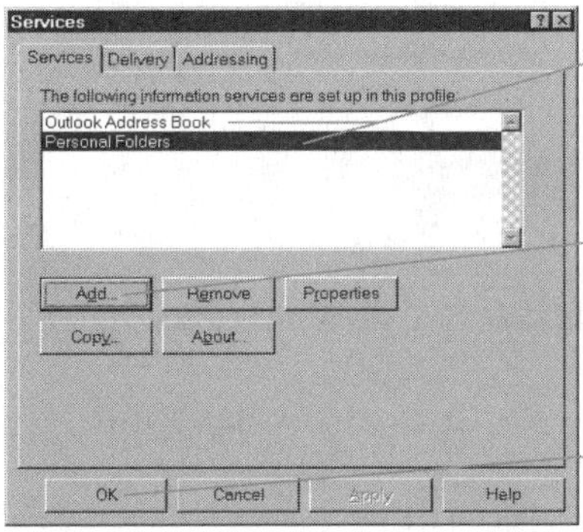

Information services already in your user profile

1 Click here

4 Click here

Re step 2 – if none of the installed information services is suitable, click Have Disk. Insert the necessary disk, complete the Install Other Information Service dialog and then click OK. Follow the on-screen instructions.

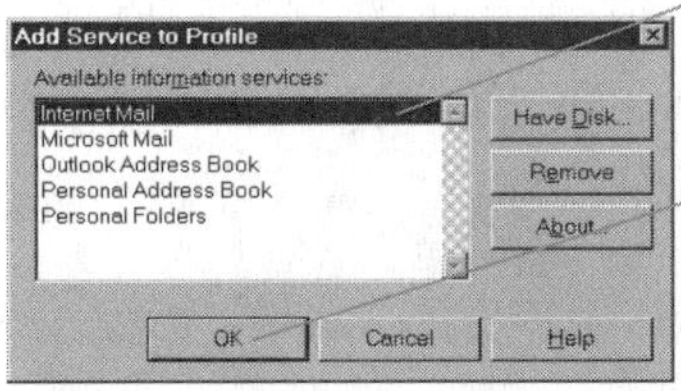

2 Select an information service

3 Click here

After step 3, Outlook launches further dialogs, according to which information service was selected. Complete these as appropriate. Then carry out step 4 above. Finally, close and restart Outlook, then refer to page 154.

Sendina/receiving e-mail

If you followed the procedures on page 153, you'll now be in a position to send and receive e-mail via Outlook. (Unless you specified otherwise, Outlook establishes your Internet connection automatically on startup.)

Sending e-mail

If the Inbox isn't currently open, click the Inbox icon in the Outlook bar. Pull down the Compose menu and click New Mail Message. Do the following:

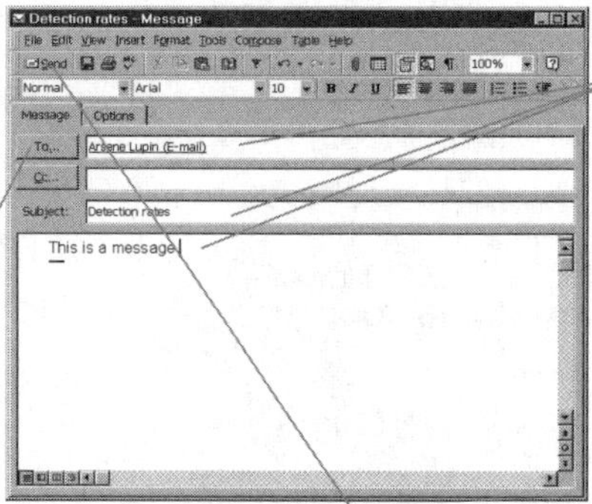

1 Complete these sections

2 Click here

Receiving e-mail

To view received e-mail messages, click the Inbox folder in the Outlook bar. Now double-click any message entry. Do the following:

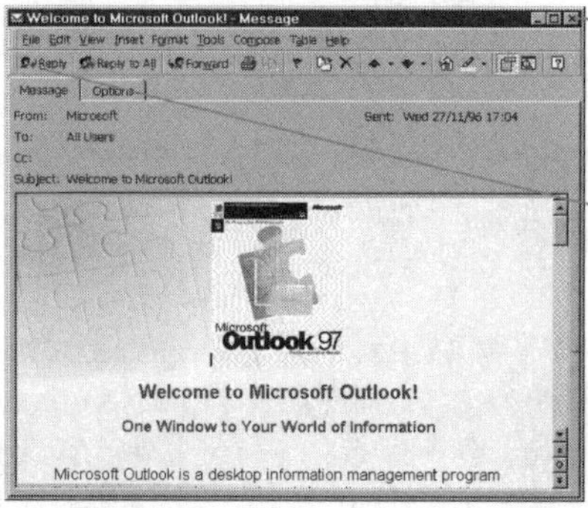

2 Click here to close the original message

1 Click here if you want to reply to the message. Outlook opens another Message window; enter your response and click Send.

REMEMBER

Mail which you've written but which hasn't yet been sent is lodged in the Outbox folder. Mail which *has* been despatched is lodged in the Sent Items folder. To access either folder, click:

Mail

in the Outlook bar.

HANDY TIP

Re step 1 – for help with addressing the e-mail, click the To button. In the Select Names dialog, double-click the correct recipient name. Click OK.

REMEMBER

You can use Word to write your e-mail. Click Options in the Tools menu. In the E-mail tab, select Use Word as the e-mail editor. Click OK.

Index

H

I

L

M

N

O

P

S

T

W